Praise for Jes

Chris Kennedy tackles Jesus' tough sayi... about some of Jesus' most challenging wor... ...ou into a deeper connection with the Savior of the world. If you crave a greater understanding of Jesus' teaching, pick up this volume. You'll walk away with a changed heart too.

—REV. MICHAEL W. NEWMAN, PRESIDENT OF THE LCMS TEXAS DISTRICT, AUTHOR OF *HOPE WHEN YOUR HEART BREAKS* AND *GETTING THROUGH GRIEF*

The words of Jesus have been the focal point of discussion and debate since He said them! Chris takes teachings of the Savior that can be challenging or a cause for alarm and approaches them in a way that not only helps to find depth in their understanding and application but makes them approachable to all people. This book will be a blessing of knowledge and growth of the Christian's life following Jesus.

—PASTOR TED DOERING, NARRATIVE LUTHERAN CHURCH, ROUND ROCK, TEXAS, AUTHOR OF *WALKING TOGETHER* AND COAUTHOR OF *MYTH OF THE MILLENNIAL*

"Hate my family?" "Cut off my hand?" "What?" Parishioners and students of all ages always ask their pastors and teachers to untangle the startling statements of Jesus. With the rod of "Context is king" and the staff of "Scripture interprets Scripture," Pastor Kennedy confirms that the Righteous One never preaches unrighteous behavior and comforts with the King of kings' forgiveness and guidance. I'm placing Chris Kennedy's *Jesus Said What?* next to my copy of William Arndt's CPH classic, *Bible Difficulties and Seeming Contradictions*.

—REV. DR. DAVID COE, ASSOCIATE PROFESSOR OF THEOLOGY AND PHILOSOPHY, CONCORDIA UNIVERSITY, NEBRASKA, AUTHOR OF *PROVOKING PROVERBS*

This book is such a welcome resource! Chris Kennedy hits head-on some of the most misunderstood sayings of Jesus with the clear purpose of coming to understand our Savior even better. This book both challenged and encouraged me. Chris does not shy away from providing some hard truths that we need to hear, yet he seasons them with grace—much like Jesus did. With thought-provoking questions at the end of each chapter, this book is an especially valuable mentoring resource for seasoned Christians to walk through with new Christians. Another great book from an insightful, Jesus-loving author!

—DONNA SNOW, FOUNDER AND CEO OF ARTESIAN MINISTRIES, AUTHOR OF MORE THAN TWENTY BIBLE STUDIES

Jesus Said WHAT?

Christopher M. Kennedy

CONCORDIA PUBLISHING HOUSE · SAINT LOUIS

This book is dedicated with love to my daughter, Emma. Emma, you are my joy and delight. As you grow up, I pray you'll enjoy reading and learning from the Bible, especially Jesus' words. Through His words, Jesus speaks to us. He teaches us and helps us to grow as His followers. Your mom and I thank the Lord for our precious little girl and want you to always know: You are beautiful, cherished, and dearly loved.

Published by Concordia Publishing House
3558 S. Jefferson Avenue, St. Louis, MO 63118-3968
1-800-325-3040 • cph.org

1   2   3   4   5   6   7   8   9   10   32   31   30   29   28   27   26   25   24   23

CONTENTS

FOREWORD

J esus Christ, the most influential man ever to live, was known to bring two things into the world with Him: grace and truth (John 1:14). His grace carries us into an eternal relationship with Him. To be in a relationship with and follow after the most influential person ever to live is the opportunity of a lifetime. None of us deserve it.

But His truth? Well, that can be a bit more complicated.

Some of His truth is easy to receive; other aspects are challenging and confusing. Sometimes, honestly, what Jesus says just isn't what we would expect Him to say.

One thing is undoubtedly true about the truth Jesus spoke: it always demanded a response. Sometimes the listeners were irate; sometimes crowds left astonished. But incredibly, the people you would expect to receive His truth often rejected it, while those who were supposedly far from God couldn't get enough of His teachings.

So, how do you respond to the teachings of Jesus? How will you respond to Jesus?

Sadly, most of Western Christianity is content to receive a little bit of Jesus' truth, but not all of it. We are content to call Jesus our Savior but resist His influence as Lord. When referencing God, the King James Version of the Bible uses the word *Savior* less than forty times, but the word *Lord* is declared nearly seven thousand times. Too many of us have gotten content with calling Jesus only our Savior.

The truth of Jesus offers us more than just a heavenly pass. He provides more than just a hope that things will be made right one day in the future. He provides a deeper, more fulfilling call to anyone who receives it. He offers us the opportunity to truly follow after Him. Today.

The truth about Jesus is that He does not offer an easy, safe, or comfortable life. His truth and the invitation to receive it will challenge anyone that would take up the call. To follow what He says always requires risk and courage. It means going against the ways of this world, looking odd, and even at times enduring persecution.

And yet, for those who take up the call to follow Jesus, submit to Him as Lord, and take His words seriously, we find in the red letters of Jesus things the world can never provide: significance, meaning, longing, and purpose.

Chris Kennedy is a friend and ally in the faith. He is not content with a mediocre, shallow-at-best representation of Jesus. Instead, he is committed to helping others understand not only the grace of Jesus but the truth that Jesus brings as well. He wants all of us to step up into our God-given identities as both adopted children of God and faithful followers of Jesus. Chris does a masterful job of looking into some of the most challenging, most confusing teachings of Jesus and helping us see God's truth in it all.

I am grateful for this work and will return to it time and time again.

So, may you be won over by Jesus' grace. May you see that only Jesus has the words of eternal life. May you be challenged by His teachings. May you receive the invitation to believe in Jesus as your Savior and follow Him as your Lord. And may you be the greatest and fullest expression of Jesus that you can be.

Rev. Zach Zehnder,
author of *Red Letter Challenge*;
teaching pastor,
King of Kings Lutheran Church,
Omaha, Nebraska

PREFACE

Years ago, in the midst of frustrating professional struggles, I sought counsel from a leader in my church body. We met for lunch. I shared my problems with him. After emptying myself, I expected sympathy. Something along the lines of, "I feel bad for you. You're in a uniquely difficult situation."

Instead, the message I heard was essentially, "Stop complaining. Keep doing your job."

The response took me by surprise. It wasn't what I expected. But almost instantly, I knew it was what I needed to hear. I didn't need to be coddled. I needed tough love—and tough love is what I got.

At the end of our time, still processing his words, I confessed, "Your response surprised me. I expected more sympathy. Instead, you were tough with me. How did you know that was the best way to talk to me?"

He replied, "God gave me a gift of discernment."

No one possessed greater discernment than Jesus. Many times, His words are much tougher than we might expect. He was no teddy bear. If you read through His words in the Gospels, you'll frequently discover a certain edge to them. To His opponents, He spoke sternly. To His disciples, He pulled no punches in teaching hard truths. To general audiences, He made blunt statements and articulated compelling truths in challenging ways.

In our culture of sound bites, it's easy for Jesus' words to be taken out of context and misunderstood.

- ❏ Hate your father and mother? (Luke 14:26)
- ❏ He came not to bring peace but a sword? (Matthew 10:34)
- ❏ There's an unforgivable sin? (Mark 3:29)
- ❏ He expects us to be perfect like God? (Matthew 5:48)
- ❏ Divorce and remarriage is adultery? (Mark 10:11–12)
- ❏ Saying, "You fool!" can get you thrown into hell? (Matthew 5:22)

These are just a few of the difficult issues that come from Jesus' words.

A couple of years ago, I preached a sermon series on the challenging words of Jesus. I also conducted a survey of my congregation to learn which of Jesus' sayings they found especially troublesome or confusing. The chapters of this book are the top vote-getters, as well as a couple of verses that I chose.

This book is written for two groups of people. One group is those who have read Jesus' words and been disturbed, upset, and even turned off by them. My prayer is that this book will help you to understand Jesus' words in light of His grace and love and in their proper context.

The other group is those who are dealing with issues that Jesus addresses but are unaware of our Savior's statements on these matters. Jesus offers practical guidance on so many contemporary issues. You don't have to wonder, "What does God think about this issue?" As God's Son, Jesus speaks with divine authority. In the Gospels, He weighs in on many matters of current interest. I pray that this book will provide guidance on deeply relevant matters.

Jesus doesn't always tell us what we want to hear. But He always tells us what we need to hear. Through His words recorded in the Bible, He is speaking to you and me just as much as He was speaking to His original hearers. Every word He spoke, in fact, was an act of grace. The God of the universe did not have to communicate with us. He chose to. He chose to take on human flesh and speak into our lives. Even the hard words are a gift given to us in love.

Christopher Kennedy
San Antonio, Texas
March 2022

Rabbi, we know that You are a teacher come from God, for no one can do these signs that You do unless God is with him.

JOHN 3:2

"A Teacher Come from God"

've been blessed with many wonderful teachers over the years. In seminary, one of my favorite professors was Dr. David Schmitt. He's incredibly gifted as a teacher—an expert on his topic (preaching), organized, an engaging lecturer, an assigner of worthwhile reading material. But to me, his most impressive teaching quality was none of the above. What stood out most was his intuition about when a student had a question. I don't recall ever raising my hand in his class. I didn't have to. Dr. Schmitt observed facial expressions and could sense puzzlement midlecture. Dr. Schmitt: "Chris, you have a question?" Me, stunned: "Yes, as a matter of fact, I did have a question."

As a teacher, Jesus regularly stunned His students. More than reading their expressions, He could read their hearts. He "knew what was in man" (John 2:25). As the Creator in human flesh, Jesus knew His audience more intimately than any teacher before or since. Because of His unique insight into the hearts of His audience and divine perspective on all matters, Jesus was the most effective teacher ever. As Nicodemus rightly said, Jesus is "a teacher come from God" (John 3:2).

TEACHER AND PROPHET

Two titles best summarize Jesus as teacher. The first is, well, Teacher! People addressed Him this way:

- ❏ The rich young man asked, "Good Teacher, what must I do to inherit eternal life?" (Mark 10:17).
- ❏ From among a crowd, someone shouted to Him, "Teacher, tell my brother to divide the inheritance with me" (Luke 12:13).
- ❏ The Pharisees demanded, "Teacher, rebuke Your disciples" (Luke 19:39).
- ❏ The scribes conceded, "Teacher, You have spoken well" (Luke 20:39).
- ❏ A grieving Martha said to her sister, Mary, "The Teacher is here and is calling for you" (John 11:28).

Jesus affirmed this title when He said to His disciples, "You call Me Teacher and Lord, and you are right, for so I am" (John 13:13). But notice that He is more than a teacher. He is also Lord. To regard Him only as a teacher and not also as Lord is incomplete.

Along with Teacher, the other title that captures Jesus' teaching function is Prophet. Luther's Small Catechism teaches that Jesus occupies a threefold office: Prophet, Priest, and King. In His teachings, His prophetic office is on full display.

At Jesus' triumphal entry into Jerusalem on Palm Sunday, the crowds rightly said, "This is the prophet Jesus, from Nazareth of Galilee" (Matthew 21:11).

Many people think of a prophet as a fortune teller. Being God's mouthpiece can involve telling the future—as God reveals it. Nathan the prophet did that when he predicted the calamity that would befall David's house after the king's sin against Uriah and Bathsheba. Isaiah and Ezekiel prophesied end-times events. Speaking about the future is one thing a prophet does, but not the only thing.

In the Bible, a prophet is one who speaks for God. Prophets spoke on God's behalf to reveal sin and summon the people to repentance.

The prophet Elijah confronted evil King Ahab and Queen Jezebel with their sin. Many of the minor prophets spoke out against corruption in their society, proclaiming divine objection to the current state of affairs. Prophecy, then, can be future tense as well as present tense. Prophecy is God's Word spoken by His chosen mouthpiece.

As far back as Moses, God revealed that He would send a greater prophet whose authority would surpass all others. God said to Moses, "I will raise up for them a prophet like you from among their brothers. And I will put My words in His mouth, and He shall speak to them all that I command Him" (Deuteronomy 18:18).

The opening of the Book of Hebrews declares that Jesus is that greater prophet: "Long ago, at many times and in many ways, God spoke to our fathers by the prophets, but in these last days He has spoken to us by His Son" (1:1–2).

When Jesus taught, therefore, He was performing the prophetic function of His office as the Christ.

KINGDOM OF GOD

Jesus taught on a variety of topics, including some very controversial themes that we'll explore in the upcoming chapters. If we're looking for one main organizing theme for all of His various teachings, that theme would be the kingdom of God. Jesus used the phrases "kingdom of God" and "kingdom of heaven" interchangeably.

Essentially, a kingdom's boundaries are determined by wherever the king reigns. The kingdom of God, then, is where God reigns in His full power and majesty. Jesus' first public teaching is noted in Matthew 4:17: "From that time Jesus began to preach, saying, 'Repent, for the kingdom of heaven is at hand.'"

His teachings revolved around the kingdom. We are to "seek first the kingdom of God" (Matthew 6:33). In some places, Jesus spoke of the kingdom as something we will one day enter, referring to eternal life in heaven. In other places, Jesus spoke of the kingdom coming to us, referring to believing in Him and living under His gracious leadership now. He also described His second coming as an event when we will "see the Son of Man coming in His kingdom" (Matthew 16:28). The kingdom is a grand reality!

Jesus taught with an eye toward the kingdom. He wanted to eliminate any obstacle that might prevent His hearers from entering the kingdom, so He warned against prioritizing earthly attachments over heavenly treasures. He rebuked blasphemy against the Holy Spirit. He revealed the very real threat of hell, the destination for all sinners apart from His saving grace.

As we study these teachings, some may seem harsh. But when we keep in mind that Jesus' overriding concern was the kingdom and our place in it, we see that He spoke only for good, never for evil. He wants you and me to be with Him in His eternal kingdom, and He wants nothing to prevent His goal from being achieved.

Because the kingdom is also realized in this world, Jesus taught about God's kingdom coming among us too. He taught His disciples to pray, "Thy kingdom come" (Matthew 6:10 KJV). His teachings reflect a deep concern for both justification (forgiveness and eternal salvation) and also sanctification (living the Christian life). He teaches us, as members of His kingdom, to live out kingdom values by loving God and loving our neighbor.

When we align our lives with God's kingdom values, God's kingdom, which is present in us through the Holy Spirit, spills over into our relationships. When we heed Jesus' words about marital relationships, we're inspired to pursue wholeness and healing. When we honor Jesus' warnings against hurtful language, we're motivated to choose words that affirm and uplift.

Jesus' concern with God's kingdom relates to eternity. His kingdom focus also pertains to our lives here and now.

TECHNIQUES

To proclaim the kingdom, Jesus did what any good teacher does: He used a variety of methods to convey His message. Here are some of His most frequently used techniques (though it is by no means an exhaustive list):

Proverbs. Many of Jesus' teachings sound like the Book of Proverbs. They're short, memorable statements, true to real life. The Golden Rule is a good example: "So whatever you wish that others would do to you, do also to them" (Matthew 7:12). The difference between

Jesus' proverbs and other wise statements is His unique authority. While others can give sage advice based on observation, Jesus' proverbs, and all biblical proverbs, come directly from the Lord who established the laws of cause and effect that govern nature.

Questions. A good teacher knows that students learn best when they're challenged to reach their own conclusions. Many times, Jesus didn't answer a question directly, which might have short-circuited the learning process. He put the onus back on the questioner with an inquiry of His own. For example, when His opponents were trying to trap Him in a no-win political quagmire, Jesus requested a coin and asked, "Whose likeness and inscription is this?" (Matthew 22:20).

Parables. These are some of Jesus' most famous teachings. Luke's Gospel contains two of the most beloved: the parable of the Good Samaritan (Luke 10:25–37) and the parable of the prodigal son (Luke 15:11–32). A parable has been defined as an earthly story illustrating a heavenly point. Jesus communicated profound teachings using elements familiar to His hearers. With parables, He captured their hearts as well as their minds.

The next two types of teachings can be the most confusing but are critical for understanding some of Jesus' hardest sayings. Both are nonliteral forms of communication.

Overstatement. On occasion, Jesus would describe an action that's possible to do but wasn't actually intended to be done. For example, He said, "If your hand causes you to sin, cut it off" (Mark 9:43). Did He want people to cut off their hands? No. He wanted them to turn from sin and save their souls!

Hyperbole. On other occasions, to make a point, Jesus described impossible actions. For instance, He spoke of a camel going through the eye of a needle (Mark 10:25). Could a camel ever fit through the eye of a needle? Unless you've seen a much bigger needle than I've ever seen, no way! In this statement on riches, Jesus was teaching about the stranglehold riches can have on our hearts apart from God's saving intervention. (More on this in chapter 7!)

THE LORD IS SPEAKING!

Jesus' message and method were always tailored to His audience. He had an original audience in the first century. Through the divinely inspired Scriptures, His audience also is everyone who reads and hears His words throughout history—including you and me! God tells us His Word is "living and active" (Hebrews 4:12). His words are not dead on a page. As we read and hear Jesus' words, our Lord is speaking to us afresh!

As we explore specific teachings of Jesus, we want to keep in mind the fundamental rule of biblical interpretation: *Scripture interprets Scripture*. Whenever we're wrestling with Jesus' words, here are questions to ask:

What else did Jesus say on this topic? In many cases, Jesus speaks more than once on a confusing topic. Taken together, His words shed light on one another and provide clarity. For instance, in the first challenging words we'll examine, Jesus says to hate your family members. Taken by itself, we might conclude that we are to act hatefully toward them. But Jesus also tells us to love our neighbors and says that everyone is our neighbor. We can avoid wrong interpretations by considering the full range of Jesus' words on a topic.

What else does the New Testament say on this topic? The New Testament contains books that the Early Church recognized as being composed by an apostle or a close associate of an apostle. These men were familiar with Jesus' thinking, and by the inspiration of the Holy Spirit, authors like Paul, Peter, and John further illuminate topics that Jesus addressed. Topics such as forgiveness, prayer, and riches are addressed throughout the New Testament by authors living in a similar cultural context. Their words help us to better understand Christ's words.

What does the Old Testament say on the topic? Jesus' words are in harmony with the Scriptures that preceded His incarnation. The Old Testament was the Bible that Jesus studied and preached. In the Sermon on the Mount, He said, "Do not think that I have come to abolish the Law or the Prophets; I have not come to abolish them but to fulfill them" (Matthew 5:17). Jesus did not override the Old Testament. He validated the Hebrew Scriptures by accomplishing God's plan of salvation as foretold. The Old Testament, then, also sheds light on the topics Christ addresses and helps us see God's timeless perspective on the issues.

By considering Jesus' full treatment of a topic, as well as related passages throughout the Bible, we can come to a faithful and faith-enriching understanding of Jesus' challenging words.

Ready? Let's begin!

FOR DISCUSSION

1. Tell about a favorite teacher. What made the teacher special?

2. What teaching techniques are most helpful for you? How do you learn best?

3. Finish the sentence: The quickest way for a teacher to lose my attention is . . .

4. What does it mean to you that Jesus is your Teacher?

5. What comes to mind when you hear the phrase "the kingdom of God"?

6. When you pray, "Thy kingdom come," in the Lord's Prayer, what are you praying for?

7. A key rule of biblical interpretation is that Scripture interprets Scripture. Some parts of the Bible are easier to understand than others. Which parts of the Bible do you enjoy reading the most?

8. Which parts of the Bible do you find most confusing?

Challenging Words about
Words about
FAMILY
MATTERS

Now great crowds accompanied Him, and He turned and said to them, "**If anyone comes to Me and does not hate his own father and mother and wife and children and brothers and sisters, yes, and even his own life, he cannot be My disciple.** Whoever does not bear his own cross and come after Me cannot be My disciple. For which of you, desiring to build a tower, does not first sit down and count the cost, whether he has enough to complete it? Otherwise, when he has laid a foundation and is not able to finish, all who see it begin to mock him, saying, 'This man began to build and was not able to finish.' . . . So therefore, any one of you who does not renounce all that he has cannot be My disciple."

LUKE 14:25-30, 33

Hate My Family?

n my congregational survey about Jesus' challenging words, one of the twenty-six options received more than half of the vote—59 percent, to be exact. Three out of every five respondents struggled to understand Jesus' words in Luke 14:26: "If anyone comes to Me and does not hate his own father and mother and wife and children and brothers and sisters, yes, and even his own life, he cannot be My disciple."

One word really makes this statement sting: *hate*. Is Jesus really telling us to hate our family?

For one thing, such an instruction would be completely opposite of Jesus' nature. Jesus is God, and no attribute is more central to God than love. The Bible says clearly, "God is love" (1 John 4:8). What could be more contrary to God's nature than hate?

Just four chapters earlier in Luke's Gospel, Jesus taught about loving your neighbor as yourself. He told the parable of the Good Samaritan to illustrate that all people are our neighbors, in need of our love and good deeds. Now, only a few chapters later, why would Jesus appear to reverse Himself and advocate hating family?

THE *H* WORD

In today's society, the word *hate* is often paired with other words to signify utter repulsiveness. We recoil at venomous hate mail. The backlash is severe for irresponsible words labeled as hate speech. Our judicial system penalizes hate crimes, acts of hostility motivated by prejudice.

Critics are known as haters.

A fast-food chain stands up for biblical values, and in retaliation, its opponents mockingly say you can now order your chicken nuggets with hate sauce.

The English language has few words as ugly as *hate*. Why would Jesus taint Himself with a word like that? Why would Jesus, Love Incarnate, tell us to hate our family? The world already has enough hate in it. Surely Jesus doesn't want us to bring such ugliness into our homes and into our most cherished relationships!

It's worth noting that Jesus didn't actually use the word *hate*. He spoke Aramaic, not English. And Jesus' Aramaic words were translated into Greek, the language of the New Testament.

The Greek word in Luke 14:26 translated as "hate" is *miseo. Miseo* has two definitions: "to have a strong aversion to, hate, detest" and "to be disinclined to, disfavor, disregard in contrast to preferential treatment."[1] A simpler way to think of the second definition is "to love less." My Greek-English lexicon lists Luke 14:26 as an example of the second definition.

"To love less" helps to make sense of Jesus' words. He's talking about *comparative* love. In Matthew 10:37, Jesus said, "Whoever loves father or mother more than Me is not worthy of Me, and whoever loves son or daughter more than Me is not worthy of Me." The pivotal words there are "more than Me." God always insists on being first above all else.

GOD OVER PARENTS

In the Ten Commandments, right off the bat, God establishes His rank in our lives. In the First Commandment, God says, "You shall have no other gods before Me" (Exodus 20:3). Martin Luther wrote in his Large Catechism, "A god means that from which we are to expect all good and in which we are to take refuge in all distress."[2]

---

1   Frederick William Danker, *A Greek-English Lexicon of the New Testament and Other Early Christian Literature*, 3rd ed. (Chicago: The University of Chicago Press, 2000), 652–53.

2   Large Catechism I 2.

Anything and anyone can become a god. We may be tempted to think that if we aren't bowing down to little statues, we don't have any false gods. But a god is anything that occupies the throne of your heart.

Can family be a god? Yes, it can. Jesus stated in Matthew 6:24, "No one can serve two masters."[3] Sometimes we have to choose between pleasing God and pleasing people. Sometimes we have to make a bold stand like Peter and the apostles, who confessed, "We must obey God rather than men" (Acts 5:29).

My heart goes out to converts to the Christian faith. These brave souls often have to choose between adhering to the faith of their upbringing and forsaking the family religion to follow Jesus. For those whose hearts are pulled in two directions, may the Holy Spirit give the clarity, conviction, and peace they need to walk with Christ. In the next chapter, on division, I'll tell you about a convert to Christianity and the friction his new faith caused between him and his dad.

No one wants to disappoint Mom or Dad. Parental disapproval stings.

Jesus Himself had to consciously prioritize His heavenly Father above everyone else, including His earthly parents. When He was twelve, Jesus remained in the temple while His family traveled home. As the family journeyed from Jerusalem back to Nazareth, they probably caravanned with other families in a large group. Mary and Joseph must have assumed Jesus was mixed in with one of the other families, perhaps hanging out with other children His age.

Then they realized He wasn't with them. (I'm picturing the moment in the movie *Home Alone* when the parents, on board a plane, scream, "Kevin!")

Jesus' parents rushed back to Jerusalem and eventually found Jesus sitting in the temple. Mary said in exasperation, "Son, why have You treated us so? Behold, Your father and I have been searching for You in great distress" (Luke 2:48). The preteen Messiah answered,

---

3   In the context of Jesus' statement, money was the god being addressed. The general principle, however, applies broadly to all things that compete for our ultimate loyalty: No one can serve two masters.

"Why were you looking for Me? Did you not know that I must be in My Father's house?" (Luke 2:49). Jesus was telling them He had to prioritize His Father over His father and mother.

While honoring His heavenly Father above all, Jesus still maintained respect toward His parents. The story concludes with Jesus returning to Nazareth with His parents and says He "was submissive to them" (Luke 2:51). He respected His parents while at the same time loving His heavenly Father above them. God came first.

HONORING PARENTS

Jesus' words in Luke 14:26 relate to the First Commandment and the Fourth Commandment: "Honor your father and your mother" (Exodus 20:12). Luther teaches that while God expects us to lower our parents below Him in our hearts, it's only one rung down! Check out some of the things Luther wrote in his explanation of the Fourth Commandment in the Large Catechism:

- ❑ "Honor requires not only that parents be addressed kindly and with reverence, but also that, both in the heart and with the body, we demonstrate that we value them very highly, and that, next to God, we regard them as the very highest."[4]

- ❑ Parents "must be held in distinction and esteem above all things, as the most precious treasure on earth."[5]

- ❑ "For to parents God has appointed and commanded obedience next to His own majesty."[6]

- ❑ Honoring our parents "is the highest work we can do, after the grand divine worship included in the previous commandments."[7]

---

4   Large Catechism I 107.
5   Large Catechism I 109.
6   Large Catechism I 116.
7   Large Catechism I 125.

The Fourth Commandment reminds us that God doesn't want us to despise our parents. He wants us to love and honor our parents and by extension to love our family members as His gifts to us. But that love must always be subordinate to our love for Him.

For many of us, our problem is not that we love our parents too much but that we love them too little. When children disrespect their parents, they break God's commandment. When adult children think they've somehow "outgrown" their parents or surpassed them in wisdom, their egos have overrun God's commandment. When adult children ignore their elderly parents' needs in their twilight years, those children have disregarded God's commandment.

We can repent of these sins, amend our ways, and renew our commitment to love and honor our parents. With the Lord's help, reconciliation can happen. The future doesn't have to look like the past. You can strive for a healthier relationship with your mom or dad, "forgetting what lies behind and straining forward to what lies ahead" (Philippians 3:13).

If your mom or dad has already gone to be with the Lord and you're feeling regret over what you may have done or left undone, believe God's Word that all of your sins are forgiven and that all whose souls rest with Christ are at perfect peace. A loving mother or father would not want their children to be trapped in guilt. More so, our heavenly Father wants to lift you out of guilt by His grace in Christ. Embrace the full forgiveness He gives you in your Savior.

GOD ABOVE CHILDREN

For some, the obstacle to fully following Christ may not be their parents but instead their children. It's hard to admit, but our children can become an idol. Some parents have forsaken church involvement completely for weekend sports. Or they've become more concerned about positioning their children for college scholarships than investing in their spiritual growth. As parents, we can obsess about our children, living vicariously through them or staking our worth on their successes.

I remember when my oldest son, Caleb, started playing T-ball. In watching his games, I became one of "those parents." You know what I mean. The kind of parent who watches their child like a hawk, pacing the sidelines, reacting to every swing or ground ball like it is life or death. Was my child an idol for me in those moments? One thing is certain: I needed to chill!

I wonder if Abraham had a similar problem. He waited for a century to have a child with his wife Sarah. When she finally conceived and gave birth to Isaac, Abraham must have been very attached to his son. He waited his whole life for the little boy. As an older dad, Abraham probably wanted to maximize every moment with his son. He must have cherished telling Isaac stories passed down through generations. He must have delighted in mentoring Isaac, teaching him life lessons. Isaac was Abraham's joy and delight.

Then one day, God asked Abraham to do the unthinkable: to offer Isaac as a burnt offering. Astonishingly, Abraham obeyed. He led Isaac up a mountain and bound him like a lamb to be slaughtered. In His mercy, God spared Isaac. The angel of the Lord intervened, saying, "Do not lay your hand on the boy or do anything to him, for now I know that you fear God, seeing you have not withheld your son, your only son, from Me" (Genesis 22:12).

In a sense, Abraham "hated" his son by putting God first, as painful as it was. Thankfully, God doesn't ask us to do anything like what Abraham (almost) did. God does, however, ask us to search our hearts and eliminate any idols from His rightful place at the center of our lives.

As much as Abraham's story is one of a man's faith in God, it's also a story of God's faithfulness to us. Abraham didn't have to sacrifice his son. God did. God gave up His one and only Son to pay for our sins. Jesus "is the Lamb who was slain" for our sakes (Revelation 5:12). Just as a ram became the sacrifice in place of Isaac, Jesus was our substitute on the cross.

TAKE UP YOUR CROSS

As with all of Jesus' sayings, His words from Luke 14:26 are part of a larger message. In this instance, His primary topic was not family relationships but discipleship. In Luke 14:27, Jesus said, "Whoever does not bear his own cross and come after Me cannot be My disciple." He then compared discipleship to building a tower. You wouldn't rush into a building project without first assessing the costs and determining if you have the resources to complete the project. You don't want to be in the middle of a building project and find out you're out of funds! You want to count the cost at the outset.

So it is with following Jesus. He told His disciples plainly that following Him would not be easy. In fact, it could be painful. Part of the cost could be relationships that we cherish. For most things, jeopardizing relationships wouldn't be worth it. But when it comes to Jesus, it's a higher prize: being a child of God and receiving eternal life in Christ.

The apostle Paul learned about the high cost of following Jesus. To pursue his calling from the Lord, he broke with family tradition, suffered physical punishment, and endured a host of other hardships. Paul wrote, "But whatever gain I had, I counted as loss for the sake of Christ. Indeed, I count everything as loss because of the surpassing worth of knowing Christ Jesus my Lord" (Philippians 3:7–8).

Here might be the biggest mental obstacle to embracing this teaching from Jesus: We think He's telling us to love our family less. Not at all! Actually, He's telling us to love God more. God doesn't want us to lower our level of love for our family. He wants us to raise our level of love for Him! And by doing so, He enables us to better love our family, our neighbor, and even our enemies.

Before telling us to love our neighbor, Jesus first said, "You shall love the Lord your God with all your heart and with all your soul and with all your strength and with all your mind" (Luke 10:27). God deserves every ounce of love in our heart and more. The good news is that not only does He demand our devotion, but He also enables it by His Holy Spirit. Love is a fruit of the Spirit (Galatians 5:22). That includes love for God, inspired by His love for us in Jesus.

FOR DISCUSSION

1. At first glance, when Jesus says to "hate" our family, what does it sound like He's telling us to do? What is He really saying?

2. When does Jesus become less than first place in our lives?

3. Some people come from cultures in which converting to Christianity is frowned upon or even forbidden. How can we pray for them?

4. Growing up, how were you taught to respect your parents and other authorities?

5. After their parents die, some adult children feel tremendous guilt for things done and undone, said and unsaid. It's important to first acknowledge that person's feelings, but how could you go on to bring God's healing words to someone struggling with guilt?

6. Put yourself in Abraham's shoes. What must it have been like to strap your only son to an altar and raise a knife to kill him?

7. Have you ever had to choose between a human relationship and your relationship with God? Share with the group if comfortable doing so.

8. Practically speaking, what might it look like to raise your level of love for God?

So everyone who acknowledges Me before men, I also will acknowledge before My Father who is in heaven, but whoever denies Me before men, I also will deny before My Father who is in heaven. **Do not think that I have come to bring peace to the earth. I have not come to bring peace, but a sword.** For I have come to set a man against his father, and a daughter against her mother, and a daughter-in-law against her mother-in-law. And a person's enemies will be those of his own household. Whoever loves father or mother more than Me is not worthy of Me, and whoever loves son or daughter more than Me is not worthy of Me. And whoever does not take his cross and follow Me is not worthy of Me. Whoever finds his life will lose it, and whoever loses his life for My sake will find it.

MATTHEW 10:32-39

Not Peace but a Sword?

I n May 2021, violence exploded once again in the Middle East. Over eleven days, missiles soared across the sky from both the Israeli and Palestinian sides. Innocent civilians ran for cover. Buildings exploded into rubble. More than 240 people died in the conflict, mostly in the Palestinian territory of Gaza.

The conflict originated with clashes in Jerusalem between police and civilians. Individual altercations escalated into large-scale violence that captured the world's attention. The underlying issues are complex and hotly debated. The deep longings stirred within the human heart, however, are simple. Witnessing devastation like that, even from half a world away, makes the heart hunger desperately for peace. True peace. Lasting peace.

As Christians, we look to Jesus to provide the peace that the world can't give. Isaiah 9:6 prophesied one who would come to be a Prince of Peace. At Christ's birth, the angels announced that the day had arrived. A multitude of the heavenly host appeared to the shepherds and said, "Glory to God in the highest, and on earth peace among those with whom He is pleased" (Luke 2:14).

Edmund Sears seized upon this promise of peace in a beloved hymn he authored during a turbulent period. Sears was a New England pastor well acquainted with turmoil, both personally and globally. After seven years of hard work for a larger congregation, he suffered a breakdown and stepped back to a part-time position at a smaller church.[8] The Mexican-American War had ended recently, and New England was experiencing social upheaval because of the industrial revolution.[9] Pastor Sears felt unrest inside of him and in the world around him. In 1849, he penned a poem that became a beloved Christmas carol: "It Came Upon the Midnight Clear."

See if you can sense the longing for peace in the third stanza:

All you, beneath your heavy load,

By care and guilt bent low,

Who toil along a dreary way

With painful steps and slow:

Look up, for golden is the hour,

Come swiftly on the wing,

The Prince was born to bring you peace;

Of Him the angels sing.[10]

The Prince is born to bring us peace. What a joy! What a relief! And then, just when we get our hopes up, the Prince rocks us with unsettling words.

DIVISION

Matthew's Gospel is structured around five major speeches of Jesus. Matthew 5–7 records the most famous, the Sermon on the Mount. The next speech, found in Matthew 10, is known as the Missionary Discourse. Matthew 10 tells us Jesus sent out His twelve disciples with instructions for their ministry. As part of this training session, Jesus said, "Do not think that I have come to bring

8 Ken Sawyer, "It Came upon a Unitarian Midnight Clear," *UUWorld*, December 23, 2002, https://www.uuworld.org/articles/came-upon-unitarian-midnight-clear.

9 Eric A. Wismar and Joseph Herl, "It Came upon the Midnight Clear," in *Lutheran Service Book: Companion to the Hymns* (St. Louis: Concordia Publishing House, 2019), 1:98.

10 Edmund H. Sears, "It Came upon the Midnight Clear," *Lutheran Service Book* (St. Louis: Concordia Publishing House, 2006), 366:3.

peace to the earth. I have not come to bring peace, but a sword" (Matthew 10:34).

Talk about a shocking statement! The Prince of Peace is saying He's not bringing peace but a sword! And He's not just talking about a sword that divides nations. He's talking about splitting a family right down the middle!

His words continue: "For I have come to set a man against his father, and a daughter against her mother, and a daughter-in-law against her mother-in-law" (Matthew 10:35).

Hold on! Doesn't Jesus want us to have healthy, harmonious relationships within the family? Surely He's not advocating that we drive a wedge between husbands and wives or incite rebellion among children or inflame hostility between siblings—right?

Other parts of the Bible say clearly that God wants us to have strong family relationships. Ephesians 5–6, for example, gives instructions to wives and husbands, as well as children and parents, about loving one another. God created the family unit and wants homes to be filled with love and unity of purpose. God wants all families to join Joshua in pledging, "As for me and my house, we will serve the LORD" (Joshua 24:15).

If Jesus wants loving families, why would He say He's bringing not peace but a sword? A sword is an instrument of violence, a tool of war. Wasn't Jesus anti sword? These words come from the one who admonished Peter in the Garden of Gethsemane after Peter cut off a soldier's ear: "Put your sword back into its place. For all who take the sword will perish by the sword" (Matthew 26:52).

As far as we know, Jesus never wielded a physical sword. "Sword" in this case is the antithesis of peace. Rather than peace in the family, Jesus would bring the opposite: division.

In sorting through these difficult words, we need to make an important distinction: division is not the purpose but the *result* of Jesus' coming. He did not come into the world to stir up dissension within families. But the inevitable consequence of His arrival was division.

Jesus' hearers were always confronted with a fork-in-the-road decision: What to do with this man and His authoritative words?

In John 7, we read, "There was much muttering about Him among the people. While some said, 'He is a good man,' others said, 'No, He is leading the people astray'" (v. 12).

Later in John 7, it says, "So there was division among the people over Him. Some of them wanted to arrest Him, but no one laid hands on Him" (vv. 43–44).

Think about the first-century context Jesus entered. It was steeped in generations of tradition. Jewish identity was central to Jewish life—the temple, worship, rituals, the Scriptures, the history of Israel.

Then Jesus came onto the scene and began calling people to follow Him. He approached fishermen and told them, "Follow Me, and I will make you become fishers of men" (Mark 1:17). Peter and Andrew dropped their nets and followed. Jesus issued the same invitation to James and John. They not only dropped their nets but even "left their father Zebedee in the boat with the hired servants and followed Him" (Mark 1:20).

I'm going to give Zebedee the benefit of the doubt and assume that he encouraged his sons to accept Jesus' invitation. But he could have responded differently. He could have said, "How could you leave me? How could you forsake the family business? I was counting on you to manage the business when I become too old!"

His sons followed Jesus. They left home and journeyed where He journeyed, leaving behind family. In that regard, following Jesus brought about a form of division.

DISOWNED

In some cultures, becoming a Christian leads to severe consequences. For some, following Jesus means dismissal from the family. Returning to the homeland could mean death.

Afshin Ziafat is a pastor in Frisco, Texas. He was born in Houston to Iranian parents and raised in a devout Muslim home. When Afshin was two, the family moved back to Iran, only to return to Houston four years later because of the Iranian Revolution.

Afshin spoke only Farsi, not English. A kind Christian lady tutored him in English and helped him learn to read in English. She gave him a book for him to practice reading. It was the New Testament.

In high school, after a conversation with a Christian friend and watching a documentary about Christianity, Afshin remembered the New Testament he had been given. He began to read the Bible each night, hiding under the covers with a flashlight so his parents wouldn't catch him. When Afshin read Romans 3:22, the message of the Gospel took root firmly in his mind and heart. The verse declares "the righteousness of God through faith in Jesus Christ to all who believe." (Romans 3 is the same chapter that drove the Gospel message home for Martin Luther!)

Afshin realized what God had done in his heart. Afshin believed in Jesus as His Savior. Afshin was a Christian!

Now the hard part—telling his father. Here's how Afshin described it:

> My father had always been the most important person in my life, the guy I'd always looked up to. I'm ashamed to say that I decided to hide my newfound faith from him and the rest of my family. I would sneak out to go to church, intercept mail from the church I was attending, and hide my Bible.
>
> Finally, one day my dad found out. He'd seen my Bible, and he'd also seen other evidences in my life. He sat me down and said, "Son, what's going on? There's something different about you." I said, "Dad, I'm a Christian." He said, "No, you're not, young man. You're a Muslim and you'll always be a Muslim." I said, "Dad, the Bible says that if I trust in Christ alone for my salvation, then I'm a Christian—and I do." My dad said, "Afshin, if you're going to be a Christian, then you can no longer be my son."
>
> Everything in my flesh wanted to say, "Forget it. I'll be a Muslim." I didn't want to lose the relationship with my dad. So even I was surprised when I opened my mouth and said, "Dad, if I have to choose between you and Jesus, then I choose Jesus. And if I have to choose between my earthly father and my heavenly Father, then

I choose my heavenly Father." My father disowned me on the spot.[11]

It was one of the most painful moments of Afshin's life. But he knew it was the right thing to do. He had to follow Jesus, even if it meant being disowned by his family. The sword of the Gospel had sliced through Afshin's family. But Afshin now stood on the side of the sword that leads to eternal life: faith in Christ.

Afshin is now a Christian pastor. He has helped plant three other churches and has equipped missionaries who are now sharing the Gospel around the world. And joyfully, he and his father have reconciled. Afshin prays for his father's salvation daily.

PERSEVERING THROUGH DIVISION

By the very nature of His mission, Jesus was a divisive presence for His audience. However, He wasn't a bull in a china shop, wreaking havoc haphazardly. Division was the result, not the purpose, of His coming. At the end of time, all people will be divided. Jesus compared it to a shepherd separating sheep from goats (Matthew 25:32). When the sword of judgment splits all of humanity into these two camps, Jesus wants the sheep pen full!

Why would Jesus cause painful division in the family now? Because He wants to save us from a more painful and eternal separation, not only from loved ones but most significantly from God! Jesus' highest priority is our eternal salvation. Nothing compares.

In the ultimate act of love, Jesus gave His life on the cross to save your soul. On the cross, as Jesus took upon Himself the sins of the world, He endured alienation from His Father, crying out, "My God, My God, why have You forsaken Me?" (Mark 15:34). He suffered so that we would be spared from eternal punishment and be filled with true peace through the gift of everlasting life in Him.

Sometimes values collide, and only one can take priority. The First Commandment says there's only room for one on the throne, and that's God. Everything else has to take a back seat, as painful

---

11   Afshin Ziafat, "Disowned for Jesus," DesiringGod.org, January 6, 2019, desiringgod.org/articles/disowned-for-jesus.

as that can be. The call to discipleship is demanding. Connecting with His statement about peace and a sword, Jesus went on to say, "Whoever does not take his cross and follow Me is not worthy of Me" (Matthew 10:38).

Division for the sake of Christ is painful, but it's a cross worth bearing. It's worth bearing because it leads to eternal life by faith in the world's only Savior from sin.

As followers of Jesus—cross-bearers—we don't seek division, but neither do we despair when it happens. In our broken world, division happens in families, in churches, in nations. When two people are on opposite sides of an issue, it can be gut-wrenching. When one group splits off from another because of disagreement, it can be agonizing. In our broken world, division happens—including division over Jesus and His uncompromising call to discipleship.

However, we do not despair when division happens because "for those who love God all things work together for good," even in division (Romans 8:28).

Division within the family took place in the early days of Christianity between two highly respected leaders. Paul and Barnabas were the ultimate tag team. They were missionaries extraordinaire. Commissioned to evangelize by the Church in Antioch, the men traveled the region, sharing the Gospel and watching the Holy Spirit bring many to faith.

Then one day, they had a big falling out. They reached an impasse. Barnabas wanted to take John Mark with them on their next trip. Paul refused because Mark had abandoned them on a prior trip. Acts 15:39 tells us that "there arose a sharp disagreement, so that they separated from each other."

What a tragedy—the breaking apart of a truly dynamic duo! After accomplishing so much through the Holy Spirit's power, the men would never work together again.

However, despite division, God was at work. Barnabas and Mark sailed to Cyprus. Paul chose a new partner, Silas, and departed with him. They "went through Syria and Cilicia, strengthening the churches" (Acts 15:41). They experienced the sword of division. But what resulted, by God's grace, was multiplication. Not one but two mission teams carried on with the Lord's work. In spite of their disagreement and separation, God worked out His plan.

When division happens in your life—in your family, church, or community—it's not over. God still can bring about good. He may lead the disagreeing parties to repentance, personal growth apart from one another, and ultimately reconciliation. Or He might produce a new relationship or a new ministry or a new movement in society that would not have happened under previous conditions.

We should not seek division. Jesus did not seek division. But we also should not despair when division happens. God is still at work for good. Because of that truth, we can find true peace in Christ even in turbulent circumstances.

FOR DISCUSSION

1. What are some of the more playful divisions you've seen in families (for example, sports rivalries)?

2. Have you ever had a serious division in your family? Share with the group if you're comfortable doing so.

3. This chapter asserts that division is not the purpose but is the *result* of Jesus' coming. What's the difference?

4. What's your reaction to Afshin's story?

5. Is division always bad? Explain your position.

6. What would you say to someone who has experienced irreconcilable division? It could be in their family, church, or elsewhere.

7. Have you seen God bring good out of a divisive situation? Share the story.

8. This chapter states, "When the sword of judgment splits all of humanity into these two camps, Jesus wants the sheep pen full!" What can you do to help fill the sheep pen?

And Pharisees came up and in order to test Him asked, "Is it lawful for a man to divorce his wife?" He answered them, "What did Moses command you?" They said, "Moses allowed a man to write a certificate of divorce and to send her away." And Jesus said to them, "Because of your hardness of heart he wrote you this commandment. But from the beginning of creation, 'God made them male and female.' 'Therefore a man shall leave his father and mother and hold fast to his wife, and the two shall become one flesh.' So they are no longer two but one flesh. What therefore God has joined together, let not man separate." And in the house the disciples asked Him again about this matter. And He said to them, **"Whoever divorces his wife and marries another commits adultery against her, and if she divorces her husband and marries another, she commits adultery."**

MARK 10:2-12

Divorce Is Adultery?

The other day I received an email from a newcomer to the church. She originally came to us through our divorce support group. She was in a dark place. Her marriage had crumbled to pieces. She and her husband saw no alternative but to divorce. Their marriage was dead.

After learning about the group, she decided to attend one of our services. When she told her husband about her experience at church, he surprised her. Unbeknownst to her, he had started watching our online services weeks before she began the support group. The Holy Spirit had led both of them in the same direction to find healing and hope through the church and its ministries.

After learning more about grace and forgiveness, the couple has reconciled. They now attend services together. My heart leaps for joy when I see them sitting together, worshiping the Lord! Their marriage has found healing.

If only the same could be said for other marriages on the brink. I wish I could report to you that every suffering marriage in my church has rebounded and remained intact. Sadly, this couple is the exception, not the norm. Too many times, I've prayed for couples to remain married, but their marriage ended. Many times, couples come for pastoral counseling as a last resort. By that point, divorce is already imminent.

Divorce is a type of death. The death of a marriage. The death of a dream. The death of a bond that God designed to be unbreakable.

No couple comes to the altar expecting their marriage to fail. But many do fail. According to United States Census data released in 2021, among American adults who have been married, one out of every three has been divorced.[12]

But the news isn't all bad. Divorce rates are actually the lowest they've been in fifty years. According to the Institute for Family Studies, in 2019, for every thousand marriages, fifteen ended in divorce.[13]

Of course, the lower divorce rate corresponds to a lower marriage rate. Out of a thousand single people, thirty-three married in 2019. Half a century prior, the number of people getting married in a year was eighty-six out of a thousand.[14] Fewer people in our country are marrying, and correspondingly, fewer are divorcing.

In writing about these statistics, I almost typed there were "only" fifteen divorces out of a thousand. But the word *only* didn't belong. Fifteen is still too many. One out of a thousand is too many. God designed *every* marriage as a lifelong union.

Jesus was unequivocal when He said, "Whoever divorces his wife and marries another commits adultery against her, and if she divorces her husband and marries another, she commits adultery" (Mark 10:11–12). The word *whoever* means that in 100 percent of cases, divorce is not God's plan for husbands and wives.

So, what does that mean for people who are divorced? I know many wonderful Christians who have been divorced. These individuals love God as much as I do. They believe in Jesus as sincerely as I do. Their faith is in no way inferior to mine. Does God look at them differently than He does me, a person who, by God's grace, is married and hasn't been divorced?

Or perhaps we're missing something in Jesus' words. In certain cases, might God condone divorce?

---

12 Yeris Mayol-García, Benjamin Gurrentz, and Rose M. Kreider, "Number, Timing, and Duration of Marriages and Divorces: 2016," United States Census Bureau, April 2021, census.gov/content/dam/Census/library/publications/2021/demo/p70-167.pdf.

13 Wendy Wang, "The US Divorce Rate Has Hit a 50-Year Low," Institute for Family Studies, November 10, 2020, ifstudies.org/blog/the-us-divorce-rate-has-hit-a-50-year-low.

14 Wang, "The US Divorce Rate Has Hit a 50-Year Low."

It's a complex issue deserving of its own book. In this chapter, as a manageable goal, we'll seek a foundational understanding of Jesus' words and His heart for people who have been divorced.[15]

GOD'S VIEW OF DIVORCE

Jesus' words about divorce in Mark 10 respond to a question from His perpetual opponents, the Pharisees. The scene is set in verse 2: "Pharisees came up and in order to test Him asked, 'Is it lawful for a man to divorce his wife?'" Jesus replied with His own question: "What did Moses command you?" (v. 3). The Pharisees answered, "Moses allowed a man to write a certificate of divorce and to send her away" (v. 4). Jesus then responded with a brief teaching on marriage and divorce.

Anytime Jesus' opponents asked a question, their motive probably wasn't pure curiosity. Usually, the Pharisees were laying a trap for Jesus, hoping to catch Him in a contradiction. To their frustration, Jesus consistently responded with "grace and truth" (John 1:14). He always upheld God's love for people and taught God's will without compromise.

In this case, Jesus tested the Pharisees' knowledge of Scripture by asking, "What did Moses command you?" The Pharisees correctly cited Moses' instructions for divorcing, recorded in Deuteronomy 24:1–4.

Hold on. Moses gave instructions for divorce? Then divorce must be acceptable in God's eyes, right?

Not necessarily. Moses' provision does not endorse divorce. The civil law given by Moses assumes the practice of divorce in society and attempts to control it, not sanction it. God desires that all things be done in an orderly and fair way. Even in the brokenness and chaos of our world, God remains a God of order.

---

15 For a more complete but still manageable treatment of the topic, please see *Divorce and Remarriage: An Exegetical Study*, a report of the LCMS Commission on Theology and Church Relations, available from Concordia Publishing House and online here: https://www.lcms.org/about/leadership/commission-on-theology-and-church-relations/documents/marriage-and-sexuality.

Pay attention to Jesus' next words: "Because of your hardness of heart he wrote you this commandment" (Mark 10:5). The commandment was not a license to divorce but an indictment of sinful humanity. God's commandments are given to curb sin, not to promote sin.

Jesus then described marriage in this way: "But from the beginning of creation, 'God made them male and female.' 'Therefore a man shall leave his father and mother and hold fast to his wife, and the two shall become one flesh'" (Mark 10:6–8). He was quoting Genesis 1 and 2. This is God's design for marriage: male and female, leaving their families of origin, uniting, becoming one.

Jesus concluded His answer to the Pharisees with these familiar words: "So they are no longer two but one flesh. What therefore God has joined together, let not man separate" (Mark 10:8–9). In most Christian weddings, the officiant speaks these words after the couple's vows. The two become one.

To signify their unity, some couples now use colored sands in place of a unity candle during their wedding. The bride and groom pour two colored sands into an empty glass container. The couple alternates pouring—she pours some, he pours some, she pours some more, and so forth—until the colored sands are intermingled. Once the sands are combined, you'd have to pick them apart grain by grain to restore them to their original containers unmixed. The two are now one.

Similarly, God joins a man and woman into a spiritual union in marriage. I've heard it compared to the Holy Trinity. In a mystery of the faith, God is three in one. In a mystery of the faith, husband and wife are two in one, so to speak. Paul, after citing the Genesis verse about two becoming one flesh, writes, "This mystery is profound" (Ephesians 5:32). Indeed it is.

In marriage, God joins together husband and wife, uniting them for a lifetime "till death us do part."

BIBLICAL GROUNDS FOR DIVORCE?

As in all areas of life, sinfulness disrupts marriages. Husbands and wives regularly fall short of God's expectations. Sadly, some of the deepest hurts can be inflicted by a man and a woman who pledged to love each other unconditionally.

The Bible acknowledges that human sinfulness can devastate marriages. In rare cases, Scripture permits divorce.

First, in Matthew 5:32, Jesus said, "Everyone who divorces his wife, except on the ground of sexual immorality, makes her commit adultery." If one spouse is unfaithful, the other spouse has justification for divorce.

Second, in 1 Corinthians 7:15, Paul wrote, "But if the unbelieving partner separates, let it be so." Many understand desertion to be a second justification for divorce. Some limit it to physical desertion; others include emotional abandonment as well. In the case of desertion, then, a legal divorce publicly recognizes a marriage bond already severed.

Some interpreters argue that these two reasons are not an exhaustive list. For example, neither statement includes physical abuse. In volatile relationships, physical safety is a real concern. As a pastor, I could never in good conscience tell someone to remain in a physically abusive situation. Abuse by either husband or wife blatantly rejects the biblical imperatives, "Wives, submit to your own husbands, as to the Lord," and, "Husbands, love your wives, as Christ loved the church" (Ephesians 5:22, 25).

Although the Bible gives grounds for divorce, these exceptions are not a *command* to seek a divorce. Just because you have a right does not mean you are obligated to exercise that right. Reconciliation is our first obligation. The marriage vows state "for better or for worse." Reconciliation responds to "for worse." Scripture declares that God "through Christ reconciled us to Himself and gave us the ministry of reconciliation" (2 Corinthians 5:18). God empowers us to carry out the ministry of reconciliation, even in shattered relationships.

If your marriage is struggling, please seek help from a pastor or trained counselor. In many cases, reconciliation is possible. Through mutual confession and forgiveness, God can work wonders by His grace.

Ultimately, Jesus wants healthy and whole marriages—a fulfillment of His original design. God intends for every marriage to be an earthly copy of the heavenly marriage between Christ and His Bride, the Church. In His words to the Pharisees, Jesus lifts our sights to God's design and points all married couples to God's ideals.

IS REMARRIAGE ADULTERY?

After Jesus concluded His conversation with the Pharisees, He and the disciples entered a house. There, the disciples asked Jesus to elaborate on His earlier teaching. At that point, Jesus spoke these words: "Whoever divorces his wife and marries another commits adultery against her, and if she divorces her husband and marries another, she commits adultery" (Mark 10:11–12).

His words about divorce are challenging enough. His words about remarriage turn up the dial on the difficulty meter even more!

Four chapters earlier, in Mark 6, we see someone doing exactly what Jesus labeled as adultery. King Herod (the son of the Herod in the Christmas story) divorced his wife to marry his sister-in-law, Herodias. John the Baptist confronted Herod and Herodias about their sin, and they had John beheaded as punishment.

Jesus' words apply to issues of His day and also to issues we face today. The relationship between marriage and adultery is an issue for us to consider with all seriousness.

Two considerations are crucial in the discussion about remarriage.

First, if there are certain conditions under which divorce is permitted—not recommended but permitted—a case could be made that remarriage after a biblical divorce is not adultery.

Second, it can be argued that remarriage could prevent the ongoing sin of lust. In the Sermon on the Mount, Jesus preached, "Everyone who looks at a woman with lustful intent has already committed adultery with her in his heart" (Matthew 5:28). Paul added to Jesus' words by writing about the unmarried and widows: "If they cannot exercise self-control, they should marry. For it is better to marry than to burn with passion" (1 Corinthians 7:9).

A pastor friend of mine wrote about his approach to premarital counseling for individuals who had been divorced: "If a divorced person came to me for remarriage, I would have a serious discussion with the divorced person about the attitude of his or her heart toward the former marriage partner and place them in God's Word. Of course, this would be handled with grace, seeking to lead to repentance and the joy of forgiveness in Christ. I think the failure to acknowledge and address the heart attitude often leads to future divorce(s) by the person."

Another option for a divorced person is to remain single. To some, God gives the calling of singleness and chastity—a noble calling (see 1 Corinthians 7:25–35). But God does not give this calling to all. God has wired us with sexual desires. It is better to fulfill those desires in a loving, mutually sacrificial marriage than to "burn with passion." As Martin Luther wrote in his Large Catechism, not about remarriage but about singleness and marriage:

> For where nature has its course—since it is given by God—it is not possible to remain chaste without marriage [1 Corinthians 7]. For flesh and blood remain flesh and blood. The natural desire and excitement have their course without delay or hindrance, as everybody sees and feels. In order, therefore, that it may be easier in some degree to avoid unchastity, God has commanded the estate of marriage.[16]

It could be argued that, for some people, remarriage may help an individual avoid "burning with passion." However, it should be noted that a chaste, single life is an option as well.

---

16 Large Catechism I 212.

IF YOU'VE BEEN DIVORCED

If you have gone through a divorce, you're likely thinking about your own history as you read this chapter. You know from personal experience the feeling of being in a no-win situation. You weighed the options and decided that divorce was better than the alternative or perhaps the lesser of two evils. You determined you'd rather suffer the pain of divorce than continue in a deeply dysfunctional or even dangerous marriage.

Or maybe the divorce wasn't your choice. You wanted to reconcile. You pleaded with your spouse to work it out and salvage the marriage. But the other person wasn't willing. The final decision was out of your hands. Without willingness by both parties, the marriage ended.

If you've been divorced, you might wonder: Am I living in a state of sin?

Yes and no.

The answer is yes in the sense that we're all living in a state of sin. No matter your marital status—unmarried, married, divorced, remarried, widowed—all of us are sinners desperately needing God's grace.

At the same time, the answer is no, you're not living in a state of sin because your sins are completely covered by Christ's blood! We are simultaneously saint and sinner, and only one of those labels lasts for eternity—saint!

Take this to heart: Divorce is an event, not a status. I can't emphasize this point enough. A divorce does not define a person. It doesn't become a person's identity. A divorce is an event. It's something that happens in a person's life.

You are not what happens to you. You are who God says you are: His beloved child.

Nothing we do can negate our standing as God's child. You belong to Him and are defined by His love. His blood covers all your sins—all your shortcomings, all your skeletons in the closet, all your decisions made in youthful ignorance, all your regrets. His Word declares to you and me, "There is therefore now no condemnation for those who are in Christ Jesus" (Romans 8:1).

The world may condemn you. Your conscience may torment you. The adversary of our souls may accuse you. God does not.

Jesus is the faithful Bridegroom. Though we've given God every reason to separate Himself from us because of our sin, He has remained true to the covenant He made with us—the new covenant in His blood, "which is poured out for many for the forgiveness of sins" (Matthew 26:28). His grace covers all. "There is therefore now no condemnation for those who are in Christ Jesus" (Romans 8:1).

FOR DISCUSSION

1. Statistics show a correlation between declining divorce rates and declining marriage rates. What effect do you think a declining marriage rate will have on our society in the long run?

2. What have you observed to be the main reasons why marriages fall apart?

3. What do you see as keys to making marriages strong?

4. Discuss the implications of this statement from the chapter: "Divorce is an event, not a status."

5. If a person is struggling with feelings of guilt over a divorce, after you've listened carefully, what might you say to comfort that person?

6. "There is therefore now no condemnation for those who are in Christ Jesus" (Romans 8:1). In what situations are those words most powerful to you?

7. The chapter states, "Jesus is the faithful Bridegroom." What significance does that statement have for you?

8. How can you pray for those who have been divorced? for those in troubled marriages? for all married couples? After discussing, be sure to pray!

Sadducees came to Him, who say that there is no resurrection. And they asked Him a question, saying, "Teacher, Moses wrote for us that if a man's brother dies and leaves a wife, but leaves no child, the man must take the widow and raise up offspring for his brother. There were seven brothers; the first took a wife, and when he died left no offspring. And the second took her, and died, leaving no offspring. And the third likewise. And the seven left no offspring. Last of all the woman also died. In the resurrection, when they rise again, whose wife will she be? For the seven had her as wife." Jesus said to them, "Is this not the reason you are wrong, because you know neither the Scriptures nor the power of God? **For when they rise from the dead, they neither marry nor are given in marriage, but are like angels in heaven.** And as for the dead being raised, have you not read in the book of Moses, in the passage about the bush, how God spoke to him, saying, 'I am the God of Abraham, and the God of Isaac, and the God of Jacob'? He is not God of the dead, but of the living. You are quite wrong."

MARK 12:18-27

No Marriage in Heaven?

Two hundred fifty-four years. That's a long time to be married! Within about a month, I conducted funerals for four members of my congregation who were married for a combined 254 years! In order of when they passed, they were married for 60, 56, 76, and 62 years.

When they died, the number stopped. As the vow says, "For better, for worse, . . . till death us do part." By faith in Jesus, their lives continue with the Lord for eternity. But their marriages ceased at death.

Much of eternal life is a mystery to be fully revealed when we are in the Lord's heavenly presence. One thing we know: Marriage ends when life ends. Marriage is not a part of heaven. Jesus said so.

He was speaking to a group of Sadducees. The Sadducees were a small but powerful group. They dominated the Sanhedrin, the Jewish ruling council. A Sadducee was usually the high priest. This elite class regarded only the first five books of the Old Testament as Scripture—known as the Books of Moses, or the Pentateuch, "the five books."

From within their narrow canon, they attempted to stump Jesus. One day, a group of Sadducees approached Jesus with a far-fetched theological question. They referred to a passage in Deuteronomy that prescribed what to do when a man died without a son to carry on the family name. The deceased man's brother would marry the widow, and their son would be considered the son of the original husband.

Using this text, the Sadducees concocted a scenario: A man died, his brother married the widow, he died, the next brother married her, all the way to seven husbands. Then the question: "In the resurrection, when they rise again, whose wife will she be?" (Mark 12:23). These men felt the resurrection was an absurd doctrine, as Acts 23:8 states: "The Sadducees say that there is no resurrection, nor angel, nor spirit." For them, death was the end.

They expected Jesus to back down about the resurrection. Instead, He surprised them by saying the resurrection is real but marriage ceases. Jesus replied, "Is this not the reason you are wrong, because you know neither the Scriptures nor the power of God? For when they rise from the dead, they neither marry nor are given in marriage, but are like angels in heaven" (Mark 12:24–25).[17] In His response, Jesus addressed the topics of marriage and the resurrection.

ETERNAL LIFE

Before going any further, let me give a brief explanation of a big topic: our understanding of the relationship between heaven and the resurrection. *Heaven* refers to a disembodied state of being. At the moment of death, the souls of all Christians go to be with Christ. As Jesus said to the thief on the cross, "Truly, I say to you, today you will be with Me in paradise" (Luke 23:43). When the man died, His soul was with Jesus, though the man's body remained on the cross. Heaven is the state of bliss when we rest from our labors and are in the presence of the Lord.

Resurrection refers to an event. The Bible teaches that on the final day of history, Christ will return and raise to life all the dead. At that moment, our perfect souls will be united with transformed bodies. And we will spend eternity with the Lord in an *embodied*, perfect state.

---

17 By saying that departed believers "are like the angels in heaven," Jesus is not saying that dead believers turn into angels or assume the characteristics of angels. The faithful departed are called *saints*. Angels are a separate category of created beings. Taking Jesus' statement in context, He's saying that as the angels in heaven do not marry, so also saints are unmarried after death.

For the discussion on marriage that follows, I'll use *eternity* as a term inclusive of heaven and the final resurrection. We'll come back to the resurrection specifically later in the chapter.

MARRIAGE

In His Word, God tells us that marriage has limits. When a husband or wife dies, the surviving spouse "is released from the law of marriage" (Romans 7:2). Marriage vows are binding in this world but don't extend into eternal life.

To put it plainly, marriage is no longer needed in eternity. Marriage has specific, God-ordained purposes that end when life on this earth ends. Earthly marriage is a copy of the heavenly marriage between Christ and His Bride, the Church. Check out how Paul segues from God's institution of marriage to the relationship between Christ and the Church: "'Therefore a man shall leave his father and mother and hold fast to his wife, and the two shall become one flesh.' This mystery is profound, and I am saying that it refers to Christ and the church" (Ephesians 5:31–32).

The most beautiful purpose of marriage is to point us to the Gospel! The union of Christ and His Church depicts love perfectly. Jesus sacrificed everything for the Church, giving His life for her on the cross. In earthly marriages, love is practiced, but imperfectly. Paul wrote, "Husbands, love your wives, as Christ loved the church and gave Himself up for her" (Ephesians 5:25).

In eternity, marriage will no longer be needed as a picture of Christ's love. After death, we'll be in Christ's perfect presence. We won't need an illustration of the Gospel. The Gospel—Christ Himself—will be ours and we will be His, which is a more perfect union than any marriage could possibly be.

Along with imaging Christ and the Church, marriage has other purposes on earth that will no longer be needed in eternity. God's original purposes for marriage—along with the benefits of marriage that arose after the fall—are superseded by a greater reality that awaits us. Consider the following:

❑ God told Adam and Eve to "be fruitful and multiply" (Genesis 1:28). Marriage is the God-chosen realm for sex and procreation. In eternity, there's no need to procreate and perpetuate the species.

❑ Seeing that Adam was alone, God created Eve so that they would be companions for each other (Genesis 2:18). In eternity, we'll never be lonely. All pain and heartache will go away (Revelation 21:4).

❑ In eternity, there will be no need for marriage and family relationships to teach values to future generations. We'll enjoy absolute harmony with God and one another.

❑ In eternity, there will be no need for marriage partners to complement each other and help each other in weakness. We'll be made flawless through the blood of Christ.

Let me say at this point: Although the purposes of marriage will cease to exist in eternity, those purposes are very much in effect until that day! Please join me in praying for healthy marriages in our families, churches, and communities. Praise God for every marriage that is filled with love, acceptance, and faithfulness. Praise God for every household in which the Christian faith is taught and practiced. We owe it to the married couples in our lives to encourage them and never do anything to divide them. Marriage is a great gift from the Lord!

RESURRECTION

While the dialogue between Jesus and the Sadducees brings up the very important topic of marriage, the conversation wasn't about marriage as much as it was about God's plan for our eternal bodies and souls: the resurrection. Therefore, Jesus took up the larger topic in a very intentional way.

One thing to know about Jesus' teachings: He always operated based on His agenda, not anyone else's. His opponents may have opened the conversation, but Jesus was going to take the conversation in the direction He knew was best. They weren't challenging

Him on marriage. As Sadducees, they took issue with the doctrine of the resurrection.

The resurrection is at the center of God's plan of salvation! Paul wrote, "For if the dead are not raised, not even Christ has been raised. And if Christ has not been raised, your faith is futile and you are still in your sins" (1 Corinthians 15:16–17).

Do you see all that is at stake? By denying the resurrection on the Last Day, the Sadducees were denying the possibility of Christ's resurrection. And without Christ's victory over death, we would remain in our sins—unforgiven, alienated from God.

Establishing the validity of the resurrection hope, then, was Jesus' greater priority.

To make His case from the Hebrew Scriptures, Jesus could have referred to an Old Testament passage like Daniel 12:2: "And many of those who sleep in the dust of the earth shall awake, some to everlasting life, and some to shame and everlasting contempt." Or Job 19:25–26: "For I know that my Redeemer lives, and at the last He will stand upon the earth. And after my skin has been thus destroyed, yet in my flesh I shall see God."

Jesus could have cited those passages or others. But He limited Himself to the Pentateuch, strategically selecting from within the canon accepted by the Sadducees and quoted from Exodus. At the burning bush, God said to Moses, "I am the God of Abraham, and the God of Isaac, and the God of Jacob" (Mark 12:26; see Exodus 3:6). Then Jesus declared, "He is not the God of the dead but of the living" (Mark 12:27).

Let's unpack Jesus' words. At first glance, it's easy to hear Him saying that Abraham, Isaac, and Jacob are alive in heaven. But Jesus is arguing for the resurrection. From that standpoint, those patriarchs are dead men. They died. Their souls live, but their bodies are dead. On the Last Day, God will make them alive again. He will raise their bodies back to life and will reunite their perfected bodies with perfected souls. Then they will be fully alive.

Likewise, we look forward to the day when we will be raised from the dead and given glorified bodies. No risk of contracting a virus. No cancer. No more arthritis. No bad shoulders or aching backs or bone-on-bone knees. No need for glasses or hearing aids.

Doesn't that sound wonderful?

The Bible describes Jesus as the firstfruits of the final resurrection (1 Corinthians 15:20). Because He rose imperishable, so will we!

GOD'S COMMITMENT

With His words about Abraham, Isaac, and Jacob, Jesus sends a powerful message about God's commitment to us. God is not content to have only your soul. He wants your body too. He wants all of you. Psalm 16:10 declares, "You will not abandon me to the realm of the dead" (NIV).

The resurrection proves that God does not abandon us. He does not abandon Abraham, Isaac, or Jacob. In your moment of loss and grief, God does not forsake you. In your day of trouble, He makes you to stand. In your time of anguish, He guards your heart and mind with His peace. The resurrection reminds us that God does not abandon us.

We hold on to God's comforting promises. Jesus said to His opponents, "Is this not the reason you are wrong, because you know neither the Scriptures nor the power of God?" (Mark 12:24). In His Word, God says, "I will never leave you nor forsake you" (Hebrews 13:5). The hope of the resurrection sends us the same message from God: "I will never leave you nor forsake you."

In marriage, a man and woman pledge to model God's love by never leaving nor forsaking each other until death parts them. A loving marriage is a beautiful picture of Christ's love for His Church.

The bond of marriage is the strongest bond between two people. The bond of grace between God and His people is even stronger.

FOR DISCUSSION

1. What's the most memorable wedding you've attended as a guest?

2. What is the longest marriage of anyone you personally know? Describe the couple and what makes their relationship special.

3. Tell about a marriage in which you've seen God's purposes being fulfilled.

4. React to this statement from the chapter: "The most beautiful purpose of marriage is to point us to the Gospel!"

5. Children learn values within the context of marriage and family. What values do you feel are most important to teach future generations?

6. Did the chapter influence your perspective on marriage in any way? Explain.

7. Did the chapter influence your perspective on eternal life in any way? Explain.

8. What about a glorified body do you look forward to most?

Challenging Words about MONEY MATTERS

He also said to the disciples, "There was a rich man who had a manager, and charges were brought to him that this man was wasting his possessions. And he called him and said to him, 'What is this that I hear about you? Turn in the account of your management, for you can no longer be manager.' And the manager said to himself, 'What shall I do, since my master is taking the management away from me? I am not strong enough to dig, and I am ashamed to beg. I have decided what to do, so that when I am removed from management, people may receive me into their houses.' So, summoning his master's debtors one by one, he said to the first, 'How much do you owe my master?' He said, 'A hundred measures of oil.' He said to him, 'Take your bill, and sit down quickly and write fifty.' Then he said to another, 'And how much do you owe?' He said, 'A hundred measures of wheat.' He said to him, 'Take your bill, and write eighty.' The master commended the dishonest manager for his shrewdness. For the sons of this world are more shrewd in dealing with their own generation than the sons of light. **And I tell you, make friends for yourselves by means of unrighteous wealth, so that when it fails they may receive you into the eternal dwellings.**"

LUKE 16:1-9

Make Friends by Unrighteous Wealth?

When Bill died at age 96, it was big news in the congregation. He was one of our most respected and beloved members.

At his memorial service, his son Millard represented the family by sharing some words after the opening hymn. Millard could have spoken on a number of topics. He could have talked about Bill's service in World War II, participating in the Battle of the Bulge under General Patton. Millard could have spoken about Bill's extensive knowledge of the Bible; he was a self-taught Bible scholar. Millard certainly could have spoken of Bill as the esteemed patriarch of the family—a great-great grandfather!

Instead, Millard focused on a single topic: friendship. Bill was an exemplary friend. If a co-worker was having car trouble, Bill would swap cars with his co-worker for a night. Bill would drive the malfunctioning car home, repair it that evening, and drive it back to his colleague the next day. The family joked that Bill would give you the shirt off his back . . . and then he'd take you to Goodwill and buy you a couple more off the two-dollar rack. (He was generous *and* frugal!)

What a blessing to have a friend like Bill. I hope you have a friend like that.

Jesus taught about friendship. His most famous words on the topic are these: "Greater love has no one than this, that someone lay down his life for his friends" and, "No longer do I call you servants, for the servant does not know what his master is doing; but I have called you friends" (John 15:13, 15).

Those words fit perfectly with our concept of Jesus. They point to His cross, where He sacrificed Himself for us, the greatest act of friendship ever. Through His Word, He reveals Himself to us and teaches us His ways. He's not a master withholding information from a servant, but a friend sharing what's needed for life now and in eternity. The hymn lyrics are apt: "What a friend we have in Jesus"![18]

Then, as we're finding often in our study of Jesus' words, He said something that seems out of character. Among His words on friendship are these: "Make friends for yourselves by means of unrighteous wealth, so that when it fails they may receive you into the eternal dwellings" (Luke 16:9).

SPEAKING IN RELATABLE TERMS

At first glance, these words seem to imply dishonesty, conforming to the ways of the world, or being opportunistic, duplicitous, or manipulative with money. Make friends by unrighteous wealth? Is the Righteous One preaching unrighteous behavior?

As always, the first step in interpreting Jesus' words is to consider the context. The words punctuate the end of the parable of the dishonest manager. Bible commentator R. C. H. Lenski considers this to be Jesus' most perplexing parable.[19] It's confusing because Jesus is using an example of unrighteous behavior to teach a lesson about God's kingdom.

In the parable, a rich man finds out that his financial manager was wasting his money. Time for a personnel change—you're fired! Before he turns in his keys, the manager quickly goes among his master's debtors and reduces their debts. He leverages his last bit of power to make sure he can justify asking for favors from his new friends later when he's out of a job.

---

18 Joseph M. Scriven, "What a Friend We Have in Jesus," *Lutheran Service Book* (St. Louis: Concordia Publishing House, 2006), 770.

19 R. C. H. Lenski, *The Interpretation of St. Mark's and St. Luke's Gospels* (Columbus, Ohio: Lutheran Book Concern, 1934), 522.

Here's the most surprising part: The rich man learned about the manager's maneuvering and "commended the dishonest manager for his shrewdness" (Luke 16:8)!

I can hear the master saying something like, "Well, I don't like how you wasted my money, and I don't like that you bargained with my debtors without my approval. But I have to hand it to you. You're a clever guy!"

Jesus regularly spoke in terms His hearers could understand, and unfortunately, we can relate to the manager's behavior all too well.

We, too, can be wasteful. We squander hours of our lives in front of electronics—flipping through TV channels, surfing the web, scrolling endlessly through social media. We allow our talents to lie dormant rather than invest our abilities to serve God and people. We spend money irresponsibly, accumulating credit card debt, living beyond our means, confusing wants with needs. We're not always good stewards of the time, talent, and treasures God has entrusted to us.

We, too, can be dishonest—perhaps not in a criminal offense but in subtler ways. We can fail to be honest with ourselves about our sins and our need to repent. We can promise one thing and do something entirely different.

Jesus, the master Teacher, knew what He was doing when He spoke this parable and its key point in verse 9. He was speaking in understandable terms, but He was not endorsing wastefulness or dishonesty.

Here's where we can apply a fundamental principle of interpreting Jesus' parables. Not every element in a parable symbolizes a spiritual truth. In most cases, Jesus emphasizes one main point with His parables. Sometimes He uses unsavory characters and questionable behavior to arrive at that main point.

For example, in the brief parable of the hidden treasure in Matthew 13:44, Jesus told about a man who discovered treasure in a field, covered up the treasure, and then sold everything he had and bought the field—presumably without informing the previous owner that the field contained treasure. Sneaky? Dishonest? Perhaps. But Jesus is not teaching us to emulate the main character of the parable. He's driving at one main point: The kingdom of God is worth everything you have (and it cost God what was most precious to Him—His only Son—to give the kingdom to you)!

As another example, in the parable of the ten virgins in Matthew 25:1–13, five virgins are well prepared with oil in their lamps, and five are not. When the five unprepared virgins run out of oil and come begging for help, the five prepared virgins refuse to share their oil. Selfish? Stingy? Perhaps. Once again, Jesus is not teaching us to imitate the main characters. He asserts one main point: Be prepared for His coming!

In the parable of the shrewd manager, Jesus is not presenting the manager as a model Christian. The guy is sleazy! No, Jesus is driving at one main point: Practice shrewdness with an eye toward the kingdom.

SHREWDNESS

After concluding the parable, Jesus said, "For the sons of this world are more shrewd in dealing with their own generation than the sons of light" (Luke 16:8).

The key concept here is shrewdness. In the verse, the word *shrewd* comes from the Greek *phronimos*, which is "associated with insight and wisdom" and means "sensible, thoughtful, prudent, wise."[20] It's the same word used to describe the prepared, or wise, virgins. It's also used when Jesus said, "Everyone then who hears these words of Mine and does them will be like a wise man who built his house on the rock" (Matthew 7:24).

In the parable of the dishonest manager, Jesus is teaching about shrewdness, or wisdom. Consider these other words and phrases that may resonate: Creative. Clever. Resourceful. Thinking outside the box. "Making the most of every opportunity" (Ephesians 5:16 NIV).

The master Teacher instructs us, "You shall love the Lord your God with all your heart and with all your soul and with all your strength and with all your mind" (Luke 10:27). Shrewd actions are

---

20 Danker, *A Greek-English Lexicon*, 1066.

a way that we honor God with our minds. As Christians, we are to be thinking, discerning people.

One of Jesus' most compelling teachings on shrewdness was when He told His disciples, "I am sending you out as sheep in the midst of wolves, so be wise [*phronimos*] as serpents and innocent as doves" (Matthew 10:16).

Normally, a serpent has a negative connotation for us. Snakes are forever tainted by the temptation in the Garden of Eden that led to sin. While none of us wants to be known as a snake—cunning, deceitful, venomous—snakes do have some redeeming qualities that are good for us to adopt as our own.

My good friend and mentor Dan Mueller explains the "wise as serpents" statement by discussing the shrewd qualities of snakes: They pay close attention to their surroundings, they're good at hiding, they don't expose themselves unnecessarily to danger, they use energy wisely, they seek out other snakes for mutual benefit, and they know how to let go of the past by shedding their skin.[21]

By referencing "shrewd as snakes," Jesus is not telling us to be slick, devious, or manipulative, just as He's not suggesting we should be naive or gullible by instructing us to be "innocent as doves." In these words, as in the parable of the dishonest manager, Jesus is teaching shrewdness as a quality befitting a Christian.

Shrewdness, then, is blameless behavior that may include

- ❑ studying how things work in the world and then using that knowledge to achieve a desired outcome;
- ❑ avoiding snares set for us;
- ❑ acting quickly to seize an opportunity before it vanishes;
- ❑ understanding the culture in order to engage it with the Gospel;
- ❑ being adaptable; and
- ❑ using the resources at our disposal for maximum effectiveness.

---

21 Daniel G. Mueller, "Aliens in Our Native Land: A Survival Manual for Christians Living in Post-Christian America" (unpublished manuscript, 2020).

Jesus follows His parable about shrewdness with concluding comments about faithfulness, including this one: "If then you have not been faithful in the unrighteous wealth, who will entrust to you the true riches?" (Luke 16:11). Shrewdness at its core, then, is about making the very best use of what God gives you—your intellect, life experiences, social connections, money, and any other tools you have that could benefit His kingdom.

BEING A SHREWD CHRISTIAN

Christians can be shrewd. God *expects* His children to be shrewd.

The Voice of the Martyrs is an organization that assists persecuted Christians. One page on their website is titled "A Bible for Every Believer." Under the subheading "Covert Operations," the following appears: "No road is too difficult, no risk is too great when our brothers and sisters are crying out for God's Word! Smuggling Bibles into countries where there is no access to God's Word is a vital part of strengthening the church in those nations."[22]

Smuggling Bibles? Do those two words belong together? If you want to strengthen souls with the Gospel, then yes, those words belong together! "We must obey God rather than men" (Acts 5:29). Through creative methods, determined believers are getting God's Word into countries where the faith is under attack. That's shrewdness for Christ!

God wants us to make the most of every opportunity. He wants us to be wise and resourceful. Even "unrighteous wealth"—Jesus' term in the text—can be a tool for accomplishing righteous work.

Money is morally neutral. However, in our broken world, money is often misused for dishonest purposes. Money can become an idol that grabs people by the heart and holds on tightly. Many people have done terrible things to acquire money. Therefore, Jesus tags wealth with the term "unrighteous." The next chapter will address wealth more extensively. For now, it's sufficient to say that God can sanctify any resource for His kingdom purposes.

---

22 "A Bible for Every Believer," The Voice of the Martyrs, accessed September 27, 2021, persecution.com/bibles.

Notice that Jesus' instructions in our key verse link salvation and other people. Money fails, as do all things in this world. But people live on by faith, and we look forward to sharing in the "eternal dwellings" with all the redeemed.

In the parable of the dishonest manager, the manager's shrewdness was motivated by self-interest and temporal concerns. In our case, the driving force behind shrewdness is others-centered and eternity-focused. We're in a very real battle with Satan for the souls of humanity. Anything we can do to bring others to Christ is well worth the effort!

In 1 Chronicles 12, David gathered an all-star army. Some of the tribesmen were renowned as "mighty men of valor, famous men in their fathers' houses" (1 Chronicles 12:30). Others were known as "seasoned troops, equipped for battle with all the weapons of war" (1 Chronicles 12:33). Then there were the troops from the tribe of Issachar, "men who had understanding of the times, to know what Israel ought to do" (1 Chronicles 12:32).

The Lord could use more Christians like that today—men and women who understand the times and know what ought to be done for God's kingdom. When we're discerning, resourceful, and skillful in spreading the Gospel, the kingdom grows. It grows with the souls of friends who one day will receive us into eternal dwellings.

Interpreted this way, the verse is one of the strongest proof texts for a heavenly reunion with other believers. Just think: Some of those friends may be in heaven because God used the creative efforts of determined believers to reach them!

FOR DISCUSSION

1. Who is a good friend to you? What makes that person a good friend?

2. Give examples of how money is used in "unrighteous" ways.

3. How does it feel knowing that Jesus sometimes used unsavory characters and questionable behavior in His stories to make His point?

4. Jesus said, "Be wise as serpents and innocent as doves" (Matthew 10:16). After reading the chapter, how do you understand the statement?

5. What does shrewdness look like in the life of a Christian?

6. Give an example of someone using money to advance God's purposes.

7. React to this statement in the chapter: "God can sanctify any resource for His kingdom purposes."

8. If you were given a million dollars to donate to a church or Christian organization, where would you direct the money? Why?

And as [Jesus] was setting out on His journey, a man ran up and knelt before Him and asked Him, "Good Teacher, what must I do to inherit eternal life?" And Jesus said to him, "Why do you call Me good? No one is good except God alone. You know the commandments: 'Do not murder, Do not commit adultery, Do not steal, Do not bear false witness, Do not defraud, Honor your father and mother.' " And he said to Him, "Teacher, all these I have kept from my youth." And Jesus, looking at him, loved him, and said to him, "You lack one thing: go, sell all that you have and give to the poor, and you will have treasure in heaven; and come, follow Me." Disheartened by the saying, he went away sorrowful, for he had great possessions. And Jesus looked around and said to His disciples, "How difficult it will be for those who have wealth to enter the kingdom of God!" And the disciples were amazed at His words. But Jesus said to them again, "Children, how difficult it is to enter the kingdom of God! **It is easier for a camel to go through the eye of a needle than for a rich person to enter the kingdom of God.**" And they were exceedingly astonished, and said to Him, "Then who can be saved?" Jesus looked at them and said, "With man it is impossible, but not with God. For all things are possible with God."

MARK 10:17-27

No Rich People Allowed in Heaven?

n 2022, eight of the ten wealthiest people in the world were Americans. Can you guess who was first? It's not Bill Gates. That's so last decade! Number one was Tesla and SpaceX founder Elon Musk, who was worth $219 billion in 2022. Amazon founder Jeff Bezos came in second at $171 billion.[23]

As their fortunes increase, are these men actually moving in the wrong direction? By their skyrocketing net worth, are they disqualifying themselves from heaven? After all, Jesus said, "It is easier for a camel to go through the eye of a needle than for a rich person to enter the kingdom of God" (Mark 10:25). In Jesus' homeland, a camel was the biggest animal, and the eye of a needle is a minuscule opening.[24] Jesus is clear: It's not going to happen. A camel can't fit through the eye of a needle. And a rich man getting to heaven? Well, that's even harder.

Jesus was speaking to a rich young man. The man came to Jesus with a question: "What must I do to inherit eternal life?" (Mark 10:17). He thought that by keeping the commandments, he had reserved

---

23   Kerry A. Dolan and Chase Peterson-Withorn, "World's Billionaires List: The Richest in 2022," Forbes, accessed July 13, 2022, https://www.forbes.com/billionaires/.

24   Some have suggested that the "eye of a needle" referred to the smallest gate into Jerusalem. After the bigger gates were closed at night, only the smaller one was opened. A loaded camel was too big to fit unless it was unloaded first, like a rich man laying aside his belongings. Whether referring to an actual needle or a small city gate, the eye of a needle was something too small for a camel to enter.

a seat in heaven. With love for the man, Jesus told him, "You lack one thing; go, sell all that you have and give to the poor, and you will have treasure in heaven; and come, follow Me" (Mark 10:21). We're told that at those words, the rich man "went away sorrowful" (Mark 10:22). If he had to sacrifice his wealth to get to heaven, he might miss out.

Here's the problem for you and me: If you can't be rich and go to heaven, then we're in serious trouble too. According to a global wealth report, if you have even $4,000, you're in the top 50 percent of richest people in the world. Moreover, if you have a net worth of $93,000, you're in the top 10 percent of worldwide wealth.[25] Compared to much of the world's population, we have a lot. We have electricity. We have drinkable water. We have heat and air conditioning. We live in abundance.

Uh-oh.

If we're among the richest people in the world, are we also among the least likely to go to heaven?

RICH BELIEVERS IN THE BIBLE

Here's the good news: Riches and saving faith are not mutually exclusive. You can be wealthy and be a believer. Many Bible heroes were wealthy, including these people:

- ❑ *The Patriarchs.* Abraham "was very rich in livestock, in silver, and in gold" (Genesis 13:2). Isaac "became rich, and gained more and more until he became very wealthy" (Genesis 26:13). Jacob "increased greatly and had large flocks, female servants and male servants, and camels and donkeys" (Genesis 30:43).

- ❑ *The Kings.* God promised Solomon, "I give you also what you have not asked, both riches and honor, so that no other king shall compare with you, all your days" (1 Kings 3:13). As one

---

25 Kathleen Elkins, "How Much Money You Need to Be among the Richest 10 Percent of People Worldwide," CNBC Make It, November 7, 2018, https://www.cnbc.com/2018/11/07/how-much-money-you-need-to-be-in-the-richest-10-percent-worldwide.html.

example of Solomon's prosperity, Scripture says that he "had 40,000 stalls of horses for his chariots, and 12,000 horsemen" (1 Kings 4:26).

❑ *Job.* After his suffering, Job ended his life with "14,000 sheep, 6,000 camels, 1,000 yoke of oxen, and 1,000 female donkeys" (Job 42:12).

❑ *Joseph of Arimathea.* The man whose tomb housed Jesus' body is described as "a rich man" (Matthew 27:57).

These people were rich *and* believers. So, trusting that all these men were made righteous by faith, rich people can get to heaven. Jesus even named heaven after a rich man, calling it "Abraham's bosom" (Luke 16:22 KJV).

Rich people can get to heaven, and for that matter, so can poor people. Paul spent the end of his life in prison without riches. The thief on the cross had nothing, and Jesus promised him paradise. Jesus Himself was poor. Luke 8:3 tells us that His female followers funded His ministry. Jesus was homeless, saying, "The Son of Man has nowhere to lay His head" (Luke 9:58).

Salvation is not about what you have or don't have. It's about who is the Lord of your life. We're saved by grace through faith, and faith is a matter of the heart. We're saved because of Jesus and Jesus alone: "For you know the grace of our Lord Jesus Christ, that though He was rich, yet for your sake He became poor, so that you by His poverty might become rich" (2 Corinthians 8:9). Jesus has stored up treasures for us in heaven. By that standard, the standard that matters, you and I are wealthy beyond measure.

So what are we to make of Jesus' words about the camel and the needle? A few verses later, Jesus shared good news: "With man it is impossible, but not with God. For all things are possible with God" (Mark 10:27). Nothing you *do* can get you to heaven. Nothing you *have* can get you to heaven. Eternal life is a matter of faith, and faith is a matter of the heart.

And here is where riches and salvation intersect. Riches are a gift. In Ecclesiastes, Solomon wrote, "Everyone also to whom God has given wealth and possessions and power to enjoy them, and to accept his lot and rejoice in his toil—this is the gift of God" (5:19).

Like all of God's gifts, wealth can be used wisely or unwisely. Consider this diagnostic question: Are you in charge of your riches, or are your riches in charge of you? For the rich young man Jesus addressed, it appears that his wealth had a controlling influence over him. He depended on his wealth more than he was willing to depend on Jesus. The man was serving his wealth rather than using his wealth to serve God.

As a stark contrast, let me introduce you to a Bible character you've probably never met before. He's mentioned briefly in 2 Samuel. His name is Barzillai. He appears twice, first as part of a group of foreigners who provided food and supplies for David and his fighting men. The other time, Barzillai interacted with David one-on-one. In 2 Samuel 19:32, we read that Barzillai was eighty years old and "a very wealthy man." He provided food for David while David was in town. Afterward, David invited Barzillai to come back to Jerusalem to join the king's court. Barzillai declined. He did his good deed expecting nothing in return. Instead, he recommended others go with the king. Before returning home, David gave Barzillai a kiss of friendship and blessed him.

Notice the difference between two rich men: the unnamed rich man in Mark's Gospel and Barzillai.

Mark's rich man felt entitled to a divine reward for his impeccable life. Barzillai did good without expecting repayment.

Mark's rich man was focused on himself. Barzillai was focused on others and their well-being.

Mark's rich man was oriented toward keeping, Barzillai toward giving.

Both men were rich, but their hearts were in different places.

JESUS' TEACHINGS ON MONEY

Jesus said a lot about money.

Many of His parables deal with money in some way—by my count, seventeen of His fifty-five parables.[26] In several parables, money is tied to bad attitudes and behavior. In one parable, the prodigal son wastes money. In another, wicked tenants kill a son to gain his inheritance. A rich fool builds bigger barns for himself, mistakenly presuming lasting security in his riches. Day laborers complain when latecomers get equal pay for a fraction of the effort. A servant mercilessly demands repayment of a debt owed to him, even after his master forgave him of a much larger debt.

Sometimes Jesus used money to draw positive analogies. He compared the kingdom of heaven to a hidden treasure and a pearl of great value. He described the angels' rejoicing over a sinner's salvation as analogous to a woman who found a lost coin.

Jesus spoke several hard statements about money.

He said money can compete for our loyalty: "No servant can serve two masters, for either he will hate the one and love the other, or he will be devoted to the one and despise the other. You cannot serve God and money" (Luke 16:13).

He said some may be enthusiastic at first about following Him, "but the cares of the world and the deceitfulness of riches choke the word, and it proves unfruitful" (Matthew 13:22).

He chastised those who rely on wealth instead of God: "Woe to you who are rich, for you have received your consolation" (Luke 6:24).

He warned against making too much out of riches: "For where your treasure is, there your heart will be also" (Matthew 6:21).

Clearly, the effect of money was a significant concern for Jesus. With the rich young man, Jesus' teachings intersected with a human being who was being swept under by the powerful current of riches.

---

26 See the Scripture References appendix for a list of the seventeen money-related parables.

RICHES AND FAITH

When Jesus spoke to the rich young man about selling everything and giving to the poor, our Lord's intention was pure. He wasn't trying to bankrupt the man and sentence him to a lifetime of poverty. Nor was Jesus trying to make the man feel bad for the sake of feeling bad.

Certainly, He wanted the young man to feel *something*. Jesus' aim was for the young man to feel convicted about his priorities. Jesus' words were designed to lead the young man to a better way of life—walking closely with the Lord and helping those in need. Jesus spoke to the man because He "loved him" (Mark 10:21).

In the story, the young man hung his head and left. "Disheartened by the saying, he went away sorrowful, for he had great possessions" (Mark 10:22). A big part of me hopes that he eventually returned to Jesus after taking some time to think about His words. We don't know. But it's a hope.

Through His Word, Jesus speaks to some other wealthy people: you and me. By the Holy Spirit, our hearts can primarily reflect Him and be shaped by Him. Riches can try to pull us under. With God's help, we resist the temptation to put our trust in wealth, and instead, we look to Him for every good thing and thank Him daily for His generous provision for us.

Like Abraham and the others who had much but trusted in God much more, we can have material goods and still subordinate our riches to our Savior and, in doing so, hold on to the gift of life that is ours in Christ.

By His grace, camels like you and me stroll through the eyes of needles. With God, all things are possible!

FOR DISCUSSION

1. How does it feel to know you're rich compared to much of the world's population?

2. How can wealth be a barrier to faith?

3. What was the fundamental difference between the rich young man mentioned in Mark 10 and Barzillai?

4. Jesus referred to "the cares of the world and the deceitfulness of riches" (Matthew 13:22). What did He mean by "deceitfulness of riches"?

5. Read one of Jesus' parables cited in the Scripture References appendix. What does it say about money?

6. This chapter asks a diagnostic question: Are you in charge of your riches, or are your riches in charge of you? How can you tell who's in charge?

7. How can you protect your faith from the negative side effects of riches?

8. This is pure conjecture: What do you think ended up happening to the rich young man?

Challenging Words about *TERRIFYING CONSEQUENCES*

In the meantime, when so many thousands of the people had gathered together that they were trampling one another, He began to say to His disciples first, "Beware of the leaven of the Pharisees, which is hypocrisy. Nothing is covered up that will not be revealed, or hidden that will not be known. Therefore whatever you have said in the dark shall be heard in the light, and what you have whispered in private rooms shall be proclaimed on the housetops. I tell you, My friends, do not fear those who kill the body, and after that have nothing more that they can do. **But I will warn you whom to fear: fear Him who, after He has killed, has authority to cast into hell. Yes, I tell you, fear Him!** Are not five sparrows sold for two pennies? And not one of them is forgotten before God. Why, even the hairs of your head are all numbered. Fear not; you are of more value than many sparrows."

LUKE 12:1-7

Fear God?

'll never forget when I got a glimpse of hell as a teenager.

At Grace Lutheran Church in Arlington, Texas, where I grew up, our youth director, Shelley, took us on several creative field trips. One outing was to a haunted house. Not just any haunted house. It was a ministry conducted by a church or Christian organization.

Inside the building, groups traveled from one scene to the next. In each room, we watched the lives of teenagers unfold. Some of the teens were the "good kids," trying to resist peer pressures like sexual temptations or drugs. Some of the teens were the "bad kids." They tried drugs, pushed sexual boundaries, and behaved in other ways that would have shocked their parents.

In the performance, several of the teens died tragically. My gut still hurts recalling those tragic scenes. Though the years have dimmed my memory of them, the impact remains.

Near the end of the haunted house, we were taken to a room of light and bliss. The good kids who died were there. They were happy and carefree.

Then we entered the final room. It was frightening. Darkness was faintly illuminated by red lights. Awful sounds blared. The bad kids who died were there . . . in torment.

Finally, we exited the scary room. Our tour guide led us into a small room with chairs. My fellow youth group members and I took a seat, along with one or two other youth groups. A presenter stepped to the front. He said the final two scenes we witnessed were heaven and hell. He asked, "Which one do you want to spend eternity in?"

He then invited everyone to walk forward to formally "receive Christ" and the gift of eternal life in heaven.

Shelley spoke to our youth group. She said that in our Baptism, Christ had already entered our hearts, and there was no need to "receive Christ" in that moment. She told us to take comfort in God's baptismal promises, trusting that by faith in Jesus, we'll join Him in heaven.

THE REALITY OF HELL

The idea of hell is terrifying. Thanks be to God, He assures us that by faith in Jesus, we're saved from eternal punishment.

Hell is such an abhorrent concept that many people have concluded it simply can't be true. In fact, that's one of the main objections people have with Christianity—that a God of grace couldn't possibly consign people to a realm of endless suffering.

In 2011, the book *Love Wins* by Rob Bell captured headlines when Bell, then pastor of a nondenominational church, asserted that in the end, "love wins" because everyone will end up in heaven, and no people will occupy hell. He claimed that a loving God and a place of eternal torment can't possibly coexist.

Not only individuals but also entire groups reject hell as a possible eternal destination. Some groups have even organized around the conviction that hell doesn't exist. Just down the highway from the church where I serve is the First Unitarian Universalist Church. One book about religious groups in America describes Universalism as "the denial of endless punishment. Its proponents rejected passages like 2 Thessalonians 1:9 and Matthew 25:46. They insisted that the restoration of all things promised in Acts 3:21 must include a restoration of every human being to harmony with God. They teach universal salvation."[27]

I wish it were true. I wish hell didn't exist and everyone went to heaven. But Scripture says otherwise. Jesus affirmed the existence of hell in His words in Luke 12:5: "But I will warn you whom to

---

27 Thomas Manteufel, *Churches in America* (St. Louis: Concordia Publishing House, 1994), 65.

fear: fear Him who, after He has killed, has authority to cast into hell." This is one of fourteen times the Bible uses the word *hell*.[28] Twelve of those occurrences are from the lips of Jesus. *Heaven*, by contrast, appears 463 times in the Bible. By frequency, we can see that heaven (or "the kingdom of heaven") was a much bigger focus for Jesus and the biblical authors. Nonetheless, based on Jesus' words, hell does exist.

The word Jesus used most often for "hell" was the Greek word *Gehenna*. *Gehenna* referred to the Valley of the Sons of Hinnom. This valley was a burning trash heap outside the walls of Jerusalem. It was notorious as a place of human sacrifice under corrupt kings. In the Old Testament, Ahaz burned his sons there, as did Manasseh. Jewish people saw *Gehenna* as the most "God-forsaken" place imaginable. Over time, the valley became an image for end-times destruction.

The other word Jesus used for "hell" was *Hades*. In addition to the word being translated as "hell" in Matthew 16:18, the word also appears as "Hades" nine times in the New Testament—three of those times from the lips of Jesus. Hades was the underworld in Greek mythology, the abode of the dead.

By using two different words, Jesus wasn't implying two different places of eternal torment. He was painting a more comprehensive picture of hell by incorporating two concepts familiar to His listeners. *Gehenna* conveyed an image of fire and destruction. *Hades* represented the undesired alternative to heaven.

Hell, eternal separation from God, is every tragic meaning and more. "They will suffer the punishment of eternal destruction, away from the presence of the Lord and from the glory of His might" (2 Thessalonians 1:9).

Hell may not seem like a topic befitting a compassionate Teacher. But ignoring hell would be truly uncaring. If hell exists—and Scripture says it does—then the most loving thing is for Jesus to warn us about it. And He does that, repeatedly.

---

28 These counts are based on the English Standard Version.

FEAR GOD?

What makes Jesus' words in Luke 12:5 especially troubling is His warning to fear the one who has authority to cast into hell. Based on context, He's clearly referring to God's authority. In the next verse, Jesus said, "Are not five sparrows sold for two pennies? And not one of them is forgotten before God" (Luke 12:6). God is in charge, and He doesn't miss a thing.

Is Jesus telling us to be afraid of God because God might condemn us to hell?

No. That's not Jesus' point here. Does God have the authority to cast into hell? Yes. He has the authority to do anything He chooses. But God prefers to exercise His authority to save, not to condemn. Second Peter 3:9 says that God is "not wishing that any should perish, but that all should reach repentance." God wants everyone to believe in Jesus and find eternal life in Him. For that reason, it's urgent that we share the Gospel!

Jesus' overarching message is to focus on what God thinks above what people think. You're only subjected to people's judgments during this lifetime. God's judgments, however, have eternal implications. He's the one to be feared.

The idea of fearing God can be troublesome. Are we supposed to fear God in the same way we fear hell? When we think about God's authority, should our hearts begin to race and our foreheads begin to perspire, as we might do nervously in a scary haunted house?

Martin Luther explains in the Small Catechism that the First Commandment means "we should fear, love, and trust in God above all things." In that concise statement, we see a powerful truth: Fear of God is always united with love of and trust in God. We do not only fear God. We fear His power, love Him for His kindness to us, and trust in Him for every good thing—all at the same time.

Perhaps Psalm 33:8 says it best: "Let all the earth fear the LORD; let all the inhabitants of the world stand in awe of Him!" We stand in awe of God's power and majesty. He has authority over all things—death and life, heaven and hell, and all else.

God has authority over all things. Graciously, the authority of God is entrusted into the hands of our loving Savior. Jesus said, "All authority in heaven and on earth has been given to Me" (Matthew 28:18). All authority is His. He spoke authoritatively. He healed with authority. His authority extends over your life—and over your eternal life.

DON'T FEAR PEOPLE

In this passage, Jesus speaks of fearing God in contrast to fearing people. While Jesus references hell, hell is not the main objective of His teaching. His point is to pay more attention to what God thinks and less to what people think.

If we back up a few verses, you'll see the situation that prompted Jesus' comments. In Luke 12:1, Jesus warned, "Beware of the leaven of the Pharisees, which is hypocrisy." Hypocrisy is acting one way in a certain setting and completely different in another setting. It's inconsistency. Play-acting. Hypocrisy is preaching morality to others but practicing immorality yourself.

What drives hypocrisy? An unhealthy concern about other people's opinions.

Many of us struggle with others' perceptions of us. In response, we try to be someone we're not. We put on a good face. You can be grumpy at home, but as soon as someone calls, you instantly transform into a pleasant person, saying, "Hello! How are you? I'm doing great!" We're careful to project a certain image of ourselves, lest others think less of us.

Jesus spent significant time telling people not to be overly concerned with what others think. We can become overly focused on what others think of us. In Matthew 6, a passage typically read on Ash Wednesday, Jesus repeatedly cautions against putting on a show for others.

> When you give to the needy, sound no trumpet before you, as the hypocrites do in the synagogues and in the streets, that they may be praised by others. . . . When you pray, you must not be like the hypocrites. For they love to stand and pray in the synagogues and at the street corners, that they may be seen by others. . . . When you fast, do not look gloomy like the hypocrites, for they disfigure their faces that their fasting may be seen by others. (Matthew 6:2, 5, 16)

Instead, Jesus said,

> When you give to the needy, do not let your left hand know what your right hand is doing, so that your giving may be in secret. And your Father who sees in secret will reward you. . . . When you pray, go into your room and shut the door and pray to your Father who is in secret. And your Father who sees in secret will reward you. . . . When you fast, anoint your head and wash your face, that your fasting may not be seen by others but by your Father who is in secret. And your Father who sees in secret will reward you. (Matthew 6:3–4, 6, 17–18)

THE FOCUSED SAVIOR

Unlike us, Jesus had a single focus. His concern was not what people thought about Him. If it was, Jesus might have conformed His actions to people's expectations. He would have declined dinners with "tax collectors and sinners" (Mark 2:15) for fear of criticism by supposedly righteous men. He wouldn't have performed miracles on the Sabbath to prevent ruffling feathers of the religious elite. Jesus could have modified His behavior to suit others.

But that wasn't His purpose. Jesus aimed to please His Father: "For I have come down from heaven, not to do My own will but the will of Him who sent Me" (John 6:38).

And Jesus accomplished His mission. At Jesus' transfiguration, the Father declared His approval, saying from the clouds, "This is My beloved Son, with whom I am well pleased" (Matthew 17:5).

Jesus stayed true to His mission all the way to the cross. Bystanders taunted Him and dared Him to come down from the cross. His commitment to His Father kept Him on the cross. His focus didn't waver even when He experienced His own personal hell, shouting, "My God, My God, why have You forsaken Me?" (Matthew 27:46).

He who has authority to cast into hell also has authority to rescue from the pit of death. Consequently, "He was not abandoned to Hades,[29] nor did His flesh see corruption. This Jesus God raised up" (Acts 2:31–32). By His authority, God raised Jesus. And by His authority, on the Last Day, God will raise all who believe in Jesus.

People may cause us grief. They may criticize us. We may feel intimidated by certain people or pressured to gain their approval. But of greater consequence is our standing before God. By His grace through Christ, we stand securely. We stand on His promises, including this one: "I will build My church"—that includes you!—"and the gates of hell shall not prevail against it" (Matthew 16:18).

---

29 When not set in contrast with heaven, Hades also can mean "the realm of the dead" versus the realm of the living. Context determines the meaning. For definitions of the Greek word *Hades*, see the entry on Hades in Danker, *A Greek-English Lexicon*, 19.

FOR DISCUSSION

1. Do you have memories of going to a haunted house? Describe what it was like.

2. Some individuals and church bodies reject the notion of hell. What's your response to that viewpoint?

3. Some have asserted that a loving God couldn't possibly sentence people to an eternity of torment. How do you reconcile the existence of God and the existence of hell?

4. The word *heaven* appears 463 times in the Bible. The word *hell* appears 14 times. Why do you think hell receives such little mention?

5. Most people struggle with how others perceive them. A few people don't care what anyone thinks about them. How can our concern about what others think of us work for good in our lives? When does concern about what others think become a problem?

6. In many places, the Bible says to "fear God." How would you explain what it means to fear God?

7. Jesus was laser-focused on His mission. What helps you to focus on a goal? What sidetracks you?

8. What does it mean to you that Jesus not only makes you fit for heaven but also saves you from hell?

You have heard that it was said to those of old, "You shall not murder; and whoever murders will be liable to judgment." But I say to you that everyone who is angry with his brother will be liable to judgment; whoever insults his brother will be liable to the council; and **whoever says, "You fool!" will be liable to the hell of fire**. So if you are offering your gift at the altar and there remember that your brother has something against you, leave your gift there before the altar and go. First be reconciled to your brother, and then come and offer your gift. Come to terms quickly with your accuser while you are going with him to court, lest your accuser hand you over to the judge, and the judge to the guard, and you be put in prison. Truly, I say to you, you will never get out until you have paid the last penny.

MATTHEW 5:21-26

Sent to Hell for Speaking an Insult?

always found it troubling that Moses was barred from the Promised Land for one bad choice.

We're talking about *Moses* here! The man God called from the burning bush. The leader who confronted Pharaoh. The hero of faith who stretched his hand over the Red Sea, parting the waters at God's command. The towering figure of history who descended Mount Sinai with the Ten Commandments.

Then, after all of that, in a very human moment of frustration, Moses hit a rock when God told him to speak to the rock. Worse than hitting a rock, Moses' greater transgression was claiming credit for God's miracle of bringing water from the rock. Raising his hand to strike the rock, Moses, fuming with anger, said, "Hear now, you rebels: shall we bring water for you out of this rock?" (Numbers 20:10). There was no "we" involved. The miracle was God's act alone. For Moses' sin, God prohibited him from entering the Promised Land.

Yes, Moses was out of line. Nevertheless, the central conundrum remains: One mistake, and no Promised Land? After all the good that Moses did?

I've struggled with Moses' exclusion from the Promised Land, but not because I suspect that God is unjust. Based on the whole counsel of Scripture, we know that God is perfectly just. His decrees are always right, whether they make sense to us or not. However, in some cases, it's harder to see how the punishment fits the crime.

Jesus' words in Matthew 5:22 may strike us similarly. "Whoever says, 'You fool!' will be liable to the hell of fire." Really? One insult outweighs a lifetime of devotion to God? One slip of the tongue merits eternal torment? In this case, too, we may wonder how the punishment fits the crime.

ESCALATING INSULTS

Jesus spoke these words toward the beginning of the Sermon on the Mount. As God's servant Moses brought the original Commandments down from a mountaintop, now God's greater Servant delivered the Law from a mountaintop. A few verses earlier, Jesus said, "Do not think that I have come to abolish the Law or the Prophets; I have not come to abolish them but to fulfill them" (Matthew 5:17). Jesus did not come to correct the Law given through Moses. Jesus came to reveal the fuller meaning of the Law.

Right before speaking this chapter's difficult words, Jesus began with a formula that He would use repeatedly in Matthew 5: "You have heard that it was said . . . but I say to you." Speaking with the authority of God Himself, Jesus communicated the broad intent of the Law. In this section, Jesus taught on the Fifth Commandment: "You shall not murder." He quickly showed that the commandment's intent is more than preventing killing.

The original Law: "You have heard that it was said to those of old, 'You shall not murder; and whoever murders will be liable to judgment'" (Matthew 5:21).

The fuller meaning: "But I say to you that everyone who is angry with his brother will be liable to judgment; whoever insults his brother will be liable to the council; and whoever says, 'You fool!' will be liable to the hell of fire" (Matthew 5:22).

In Jesus' words, some see a gradation of sins and punishments. Those who hold this view suggest that in Jesus' three groupings of offenses and consequences, the first is somewhat minor, the second is more severe, and the third is worst of all.

The first sin is anger toward your brother. This could be understood as anger in the heart expressed in a small way—a sideways glance, a roll of the eyes, muttering under the breath. The same Greek word for anger shows up in Ephesians 4:26: "Be angry and do not sin; do not let the sun go down on your anger." Anger is a God-given emotion. Emotions in themselves are not sins. But thoughts and actions that come from those emotions can be sinful.

According to Jesus' words, anger toward your brother deserves judgment. The word translated as "judgment" could also be used to refer to a specific group of judges, such as a local tribunal. The passage then could be understood to mean that if you express anger sinfully toward your brother, you'll be answerable to the lower court.

The second sin in the grouping is insulting your brother. The ESV footnote provides the Aramaic word *raca*, a term of abuse. Its root meaning is "empty." The insult would be something like, "You empty-headed man!" or "You numbskull!"

Whereas anger toward your brother is matched with judgment, perhaps a lower court, *raca* receives a harsher sentence. "Council" is the Greek word *synedrion*, or Sanhedrin. The Sanhedrin was the Supreme Court of Jewish society. Imagine calling someone a knucklehead, then having to answer to the Supreme Court!

The third sin is "You fool!" It's interesting to note that calling someone a fool isn't completely out of bounds in the Bible. The psalmist wrote, "The fool says in his heart, 'There is no God'" (Psalm 53:1). Jesus Himself said to the scribes and Pharisees, "You blind fools!" (Matthew 23:17). The Greek word here is *moros*, from which we get the English word *moron*. Commentator William Barclay writes that a *moros* was a moral fool. Such an insult would have reputation-destroying force.[30] The word didn't only imply intellectual deficiency. It also had "the connotation of an obstinate, godless person."[31]

For the severest expression of anger—calling into question someone's morals or even faith—the severest punishment is reserved: hell itself.

---

30 William Barclay, *The Gospel of Matthew*, vol. 1, 2nd ed. (Philadelphia: The Westminster Press, 1958), 137.

31 Danker, *A Greek-English Lexicon*, 663.

ROOT OF ANGER

An examination of the gradation theory is useful for exploring the words and movement of the text. It makes sense. When it comes to consequences in this world, we can understand that more severe crimes receive more devastating punishments. As He often did, Jesus taught using concepts that were easily relatable.

Having said that, a larger message emerges from these challenging words. Jesus has grander goals than to give us neat and tidy categories for our sins. He doesn't want us to measure our sins and choose the lesser sins to avoid harsher punishment. He wants all sin in our lives to be overcome by the Gospel!

For the Gospel to have its full impact on the human heart, Jesus confronts us with the Law in all its power. In our world of cause and effect, sin deserves punishment. God's Law demands it.

How our sins relate to God's Law differs from how our sins relate to societal laws. According to the laws of government, different sins deserve different punishments. Some transgressions result in a ticket and a fine; others get you a night in jail. For a society to function properly, laws and corresponding consequences must be in place.

God's Law operates on a different plane. According to God's Law, all sin warrants one punishment: eternal separation from God. By definition, this is hell (a concept explored more fully in the previous chapter).

At the root of both murder and insults lies the same core problem: our sin. We might think, as Jesus' original audience might have thought, that murder is much worse than an insult. On one level, murder is worse because it ends one life and devastates the lives of everyone who loved the victim. Human laws punish sins according to their effect on personal lives and society.

On another level, murder and insults share the same problem. They both grow from the same bitter root. They both reveal a problem of the heart. Jesus puts it plainly: "For out of the abundance of the heart the mouth speaks" (Matthew 12:34).

Because sin is a matter of the heart, any sin, even the "smallest" one, is enough to separate us from God eternally. Therefore, all sin needs to be addressed. For every sin, "big" and "small," the Law drives us to our knees before God in repentance, seeking His grace through Jesus, whose blood was spilled as a sacrifice for all sins.

FORGIVING OUR WORDS

Angry words inflamed and hastened the circumstances resulting in Jesus' crucifixion.

Jesus' accusers insulted Him with lies about His actions and motives: "We found this man misleading our nation and forbidding us to give tribute to Caesar" (Luke 23:2).

They insulted Him with sarcasm: "Hail, King of the Jews!" (John 19:3).

They insulted Him by mocking His prophetic office, blindfolding Him, beating Him, and saying, "Prophesy! Who is it that struck You?" (Luke 22:64).

Those who insulted Him are just as guilty as those who nailed Him to the cross. Likewise, our insults and angry words make us guilty before God, just as the highest capital offense would condemn us before God. Because of our sins, we deserve the fire of hell.

But thanks be to God! Through faith in Jesus, our sins of word are just as forgiven as our sins of deed, and we are guaranteed the joys of heaven!

If you doubt that your worst deeds are forgiven, consider the thief on the cross. He admitted that his execution was just, saying to the other thief, "We are receiving the due reward of our deeds" (Luke 23:41). Whatever crime he committed, he earned the death penalty according to Roman law. Yet when the thief appealed to Jesus, the Savior promised, "Truly, I say to you, today you will be with Me in paradise" (Luke 23:43). Your worst actions can't outweigh His immeasurable grace.

Neither can your worst words. Look at the apostle Paul, a former opponent of the Church who became its greatest missionary. He wrote to the young pastor Timothy, "Formerly I was a blasphemer, persecutor, and insolent opponent. But I received mercy because

I had acted ignorantly in unbelief, and the grace of our Lord overflowed for me with the faith and love that are in Christ Jesus" (1 Timothy 1:13–14). Paul's words and deeds were forgiven as God's love overflowed for him through Jesus!

The same is true for you!

GOOD WORDS

God's Law confronts us in a threefold way. It curbs our sin: "Don't do that!" It confronts us, showing our desperate need for a Savior: "Repent and believe!" And it teaches us how to live a sanctified life: "Do this!"

Jesus' words in Matthew 5 direct us to the third use of the Law, sanctified living. For everything that Jesus forbids, He also teaches us about the shape of the Christian life. Consider Jesus' words after our key verse: "So if you are offering your gift at the altar and there remember that your brother has something against you, leave your gift there before the altar and go. First be reconciled to your brother, and then come and offer your gift" (Matthew 5:23–24). How is one person to be reconciled to another? Most often, with words! Just as words can have destructive force, they also can restore.

A church member told me about the time he was walking to his car when another member pulled up next to him and got out of her car. She had formed a negative opinion of him based on a past event. As she observed more of his actions and saw the love he exuded for people, she discovered that her initial impression was wrong. "I'm sorry," she said to him that day in the parking lot. "I didn't know you. Now I do."

He had no idea how she felt about him previously. It wasn't on his radar at all. But before she exited the parking lot, she had some reconciling to do in her own heart. And to accomplish her goal, she used words. Words of apology and words of affirmation.

Just as a heart filled with anger can overflow destructively with insults, so also a heart of grace can overflow with words of healing and love. In His tough words to us, Jesus is by no means seeking to silence us completely. He wants to replace hurtful words from an angry heart with uplifting words from a joyful heart!

I heard this saying many times growing up: "If you can't say anything nice, don't say anything at all." (I'm not sure why my mom thought I needed to hear that so often!) While the saying is true and wise, a greater challenge is to find something nice to say!

Ephesians 4:29 beautifully captures the speech God desires from us: "Let no corrupting talk come out of your mouths, but only such as is good for building up, as fits the occasion, that it may give grace to those who hear."

With your words, you can give grace to those who hear!

FOR DISCUSSION

1. When you think of a "fool," what comes to mind?

2. Read Psalm 53. How does the psalm depict a fool?

3. What's your response to the gradation theory about Jesus' words in Matthew 5:22?

4. The chapter states, "Those who insulted Him are just as guilty as those who nailed Him to the cross." Do you agree or disagree? Explain your answer.

5. What tends to push your buttons and anger you?

6. What helps you control your anger?

7. "If you can't say anything nice, don't say anything at all." Sometimes it's best to say nothing. When is that hardest to do?

8. The chapter states, "He wants to replace hurtful words from an angry heart with uplifting words from a joyful heart!" Think of uplifting words you might say to someone this week. Share with the group.

Whoever causes one of these little ones who believe in Me to sin, it would be better for him if a great millstone were hung around his neck and he were thrown into the sea. And **if your hand causes you to sin, cut it off. It is better for you to enter life crippled than with two hands to go to hell, to the unquenchable fire. And if your foot causes you to sin, cut it off. It is better for you to enter life lame than with two feet to be thrown into hell. And if your eye causes you to sin, tear it out. It is better for you to enter the kingdom of God with one eye than with two eyes to be thrown into hell,** "where their worm does not die and the fire is not quenched." For everyone will be salted with fire. Salt is good, but if the salt has lost its saltiness, how will you make it salty again? Have salt in yourselves, and be at peace with one another.

MARK 9:42–50

Cut Off Your Hand?

I n February 2021, my fellow Texans and I endured historic winter storms. The storms were nicknamed Snowpocalypse or Snowmaggedon. The region was unprepared to handle the intensity of the storms, and as a result, many Texans went without power.

While the temperatures remained subfreezing, I was responsible for checking on my neighbors' house each day. The house was unoccupied at the time. My neighbors, in their nineties, were both in a medical facility as they recovered from health issues.

On one of those cold days, my two oldest boys, Caleb and Ethan, walked with me to the neighbors' house. The ground was covered in thick snow. Thinking I was stepping from the street onto the driveway, I actually stepped onto the edge of the curb. My feet slid out from under me, and I began to fall backward. Fortunately, with catlike reflexes (ha!), I was able to catch myself and avoid injury.

Watch your step!

Along with concern for our physical safety, God desires spiritual safety for us. And so in His Word, He teaches us to guard ourselves against slippery sins. Jesus warned against bad actions that cascade downward into devastating consequences.

Repeatedly in Mark 9:43–48, Jesus cautions against sin. In the Greek New Testament, the most common word for sin is *hamartia*, which means "to miss the mark," like an archer missing the target.[32] The word Jesus uses here is different. The Greek is *skandalidzo*. It

---

32 See W. E. Vine, *An Expository Dictionary of New Testament Words* (Nashville: Thomas Nelson Publishers, 1952), 1045.

appears far less often and literally means "to stumble" or "to cause to fall."[33] Jesus warns against falling into sin or causing others to fall into sin. He's shouting to us: "Watch your step!"

To emphasize His point, Jesus chose strong language: "If your hand causes you to sin, cut it off. . . . If your foot causes you to sin, cut it off. . . . If your eye causes you to sin, tear it out" (vv. 43, 45, 47). Is Jesus telling us to hurt ourselves? Is this His prescription for curbing our sinful impulses?

In 2011, this literally happened. Aldo Bianchini, a forty-six-year-old man, was attending a church service in northern Italy. According to news reports, he began to mutilate his own eyes in the middle of the service. I'll spare you the gory details. No doubt mentally disturbed, he said voices in his head told him to do it.[34]

Please do not respond to any of Jesus' words by physically harming yourself! Remember, Jesus sometimes spoke in nonliteral forms of communication: overstatement and hyperbole. These words from Mark 9 would be considered an overstatement, an action that's possible to do but wasn't actually intended to be done.

Such shocking words function as a flashing neon sign: Watch your step! Jesus' message was so important that He chose the most arresting language possible to grab attention and sear His words into people's memories. It worked, didn't it?

Our eyes, hands, and feet can lead us into slippery sins. With our eyes, we can look at images that stir up lust in our hearts. With our hands, we can take what's not ours. With our feet, we can go places we shouldn't go. We can commit seemingly innocent, minor infractions. Just a glance at a picture. Just a handful of what isn't mine. Just a couple of minutes in the wrong place. Little things.

But with God, no sins are little. All sin separates us from Him. Hebrews 3 warns against "the deceitfulness of sin" (v. 13). James 1 says, "Each person is tempted when he is lured and enticed by his own desire. Then desire when it has conceived gives birth to sin, and

---

33 See Vine, *An Expository Dictionary of New Testament Words*, 802.

34 "Aldo Bianchini, Viareggio Man, Rips His Own Eyeballs Out during Church Service," *Huffpost*, updated December 3, 2011, https://www.huffpost.com/entry/aldo-bianchini-tears-eyes-church_n_992108.

sin when it is fully grown brings forth death" (vv. 14–15). A little desire leads to sin, and sin leads to death.

You and I know from personal experience that sin can be slippery. A bad habit leads to addiction. An isolated incident becomes a pattern. Sinful behavior, left unchecked, can spiral out of control.

Because we have sinned with our eyes, hands, and feet, Jesus suffered. His eyes were stung by sweat and blood pouring down from His thorn-pierced head. His hands were pierced by metal spikes. His feet likewise were nailed to the cross.

Why? Because of our sins, big and little.

Why? Because He loves us.

Why? Because only through the sacrifice of Christ are we fully reconciled with God.

RIGHTEOUS ALTERNATIVES

Jesus has paid for your sins, and He strengthens you to stand against temptation to sin. In His Word, God provides righteous alternatives for your eyes, hands, and feet.

In Philippians 3:17, Paul wrote, "Brothers, join in imitating me, and keep your eyes on those who walk according to the example you have in us." Rather than allowing our eyes to be fixed on unholy images, God invites us to watch and learn from holy people. As we hang around people who desire to live for God, we pick up on their habits. What we observe with our eyes, we imitate with our lives.

In Deuteronomy 15, God says, "You shall open wide your hand to your brother, to the needy and to the poor, in your land" (v. 11). Instead of holding on tightly to everything we have, God's Word teaches us to be generous, to let go, to give with an open hand. Our hands are for serving.

In Romans 10:15, God declares that He gives you beautiful feet to deliver the message of the Savior's love. With feet sanctified by the Savior's blood, we can go to the needy, the stranger, the lonely, and the lost. Wherever our feet take us, we're ambassadors of grace. We go with our feet to make disciples (Matthew 28:19).

The best way to avoid doing bad actions is to occupy yourself with good actions. Ever heard of Frank Abagnale? Frank was the subject of the 2002 movie *Catch Me If You Can*, starring Leonardo DiCaprio and Tom Hanks. The movie is based on the real-life odyssey of a young man who became an expert at deception. First, in the movie, he impersonates a pilot and forges payroll checks worth millions. After that, Frank poses as a doctor. Then he reassumes his false identity as a pilot, successfully escapes from the authorities by flying to Spain, and makes his home in Europe.

Frank is really good at doing really bad things.

Eventually, his crimes catch up to him. In the movie, Carl Hanratty, an FBI agent, tracks down Frank, arrests him, and brings him back to the United States. Frank is sentenced to twelve years in a maximum-security prison.

Then, at the end, the plot takes a very positive twist. One day, Carl brings a forged check to Frank and asks for his advice. Using his knowledge as an experienced forger, Frank helps Carl crack the case and identify the culprit. After that, Frank has a job. He begins working for the FBI bank fraud unit. From that point forward, he's able to avoid doing bad actions by occupying himself with good actions.

OUR MOTIVATION

The motivation to live holy lives is more than staying out of trouble or self-preservation. Our calling as Christians is not merely avoidance of sin. We're not just trying to "keep out of hell." All who trust in Christ are heaven-bound and are entrusted with bringing His values into this world until we arrive in His eternal kingdom.

The motivation for holy living also is not only for ourselves. Jesus teaches us these things for our sake *and* for the benefit of others. Shortly before our text, Jesus took a child in His arms and spoke about receiving a child in His name (Mark 9:37). Then, in the opening verses of our text, Jesus said, "Whoever causes one of these little ones who believe in Me to sin, it would be better for him if a great millstone were hung around his neck and he were thrown into the sea" (Mark 9:42).

It's one thing for you to stumble. It's another thing for you to fall and take someone down with you—especially someone weaker, more impressionable, more vulnerable. When I had my near-fall on the icy sidewalk, the only thing worse than me slipping and falling would have been me going down and taking my boys down with me, possibly injuring them.

The "little one" could be a child. It could be a new Christian, someone weak in their faith, or someone who's struggling to maintain hope. As believers, we are to set a Christlike example to others.

In Romans 15:1, God says to us, "We who are strong have an obligation to bear with the failings of the weak, and not to please ourselves." We have an obligation to those who are weaker than us. Leading them into sin is an enormous tragedy, an abuse of our influence. By our example, we're able to lead people into godly living. What people observe, they imitate.

We are to be reflections of Christ to the world no matter the circumstance. Guided by the Holy Spirit, we can keep our spiritual footing and move forward. As we walk in step with the Spirit, God guides our feet—and our hands and our eyes—to live to His glory.

FOR DISCUSSION

1. Tell about the worst winter storm you've experienced. Did you find yourself more aware of watching your step when you went outside?

2. The Bible warns us to watch our step spiritually with some rather strong language. How does it strike you to read such strong language from Jesus, saying to cut off your hand or foot and to tear out your eye?

3. When are you tempted to dismiss something as a "little sin"?

4. React to how Frank Abagnale's story turned out. What hope does his turnaround give you for yourself or others?

5. What actions do you feel are most likely to cause "little ones" to stumble?

6. This chapter states, "All who trust in Christ are heaven-bound and are entrusted with bringing His values into this world until we arrive in His eternal kingdom." What are those values? How do we bring His values into this world?

7. This chapter states, "What people observe, they imitate." Have you found this to be true? Share an example.

8. This week, what is something God-honoring you can do with your eyes, hands, or feet?

And when you pray, do not heap up empty phrases as the Gentiles do, for they think that they will be heard for their many words. Do not be like them, for your Father knows what you need before you ask Him. Pray then like this: Our Father in heaven, hallowed be Your name. Your kingdom come, Your will be done, on earth as it is in heaven. Give us this day our daily bread, and forgive us our debts, as we also have forgiven our debtors. And lead us not into temptation, but deliver us from evil. **For if you forgive others their trespasses, your heavenly Father will also forgive you, but if you do not forgive others their trespasses, neither will your Father forgive your trespasses.**

MATTHEW 6:7–15

No Forgiveness for the Unforgiving?

T his is a book about words Jesus spoke. A book also could be written about words Jesus did *not* speak, statements like "Love the sinner; hate the sin," or "God helps those who help themselves." Some people assume those words are biblical, but they're not found on Jesus' lips or elsewhere in the Bible.

Other words Jesus probably didn't say: "For Thine is the kingdom and the power and the glory forever and ever. Amen."

You may be thinking: "Hold on a second! That's part of the Lord's Prayer. And it's called the *Lord's* Prayer because the Lord Jesus spoke it!"

In most English Bibles, the familiar conclusion we speak to the Lord's Prayer is a footnote for Matthew 6:13, not part of the main text. Scholars believe the phrase was formulated centuries after the New Testament was written as an eloquent way to end the prayer.[35]

Our beloved version of the Lord's Prayer ends with the beautiful doxology (words of praise): "For Thine is the kingdom and the power and the glory forever and ever. Amen." But when Jesus taught the Lord's Prayer, He finished the prayer not with a doxology but with words of *challenge*. With the doxology, we wrap a neat, tidy bow

---

35 See the note on Matthew 6:13 in *The Lutheran Study Bible* (St. Louis: Concordia Publishing House, 2009).

on the end of the prayer. Jesus, on the other hand, left the prayer open-ended with a call to action.

Rather than end the prayer and begin a new topic, Jesus revisited the Fifth Petition: "And forgive us our debts, as we also have forgiven our debtors. And lead us not into temptation, but deliver us from evil. For if you forgive others their trespasses, your heavenly Father will also forgive you, but if you do not forgive others their trespasses, neither will your Father forgive your trespasses" (Matthew 6:13–15).

The prayer has ended, but the work has only begun.

Forgiving others is one of the most difficult demands of discipleship, but it's an essential part of Christian living. Because of the cross, where God forgives our sins in Christ, we know that forgiveness is at the heart of the Christian faith. So, Jesus returns to the topic right after the prayer.

Forgiveness is so important it requires extra emphasis.

THE CHALLENGE OF FORGIVENESS

Jesus' words about forgiveness have alarmed many. He seems to be saying that if you forgive, God will forgive you, and if you hold onto a grudge, God will retain your sins.

Is that what Jesus means? Is that really how it works?

First, we should define what forgiveness is. The New Testament Greek word most often used for "forgive" is *aphiemi*. This is the word in Matthew 6. At a root level, *aphiemi* contains a meaning of dismissing, releasing, letting go, sending away. In the context of Matthew 6, dealing with how to respond to sins, *aphiemi* means "to release from legal or moral obligation or consequence; cancel, remit, pardon."[36]

You forgive a loan or a debt. You wipe it out so the other person is no longer obligated. Forgiveness of sins is a similar idea. When you forgive someone, you cancel the debt. You release the other person. You let go. You send the sin away. You grant a complete pardon.

---

36   Danker, *A Greek-English Lexicon*, 156.

God does that for us in Jesus. God deals with our sins through the cross. Jesus suffered for our sins, and by faith in His completed work, the words of Psalm 103:12 are true for us: "As far as the east is from the west, so far does He remove our transgressions from us."

Thanks be to God for His gift of forgiveness!

And that's where the dilemma of Matthew 6:14–15 arises. It appears to call into question God's gift of forgiveness. If our forgiveness before God is conditional, based on our ability to forgive others, we may be in serious trouble! You and I sometimes struggle to forgive others.

People do bad things to one another. Maybe people have done bad things to you. It's hard to just "get over it."

A doctor may have mistreated your loved one, causing permanent damage. Ever since, you've felt nothing but disdain for that doctor.

Someone may have humiliated you. Words sting. Hurtful words can become lodged in your mind, and with them, a grudge takes up permanent residence in your heart.

A person you once trusted may have betrayed your trust. You may have given money or your heart, only to be stabbed in the back.

Perhaps you've been a victim of sexual abuse. Or emotional abuse. Or infidelity.

These are not minor infractions. These are deeply painful episodes with long-term consequences. They leave scars.

If you struggle to forgive others, will God retain your sins? Will your failure to overcome the past jeopardize your eternal salvation?

GOD'S FORGIVENESS AND OURS

Let's be clear about one thing: Salvation is a gift. We can't earn it. We can reject God's love, but we can't earn forgiveness by forgiving others. God's forgiveness always precedes ours. He forgives you on account of Christ, not on account of anything you do.

Jesus taught the Lord's Prayer as part of the Sermon on the Mount. The sermon was preached to believers, to people earnestly seeking to follow Jesus. These words were not spoken to the Pharisees or scribes who were constantly challenging Him. Jesus addressed these words to His disciples and people who joined the disciples to hear Jesus.

The King was addressing residents of His kingdom. He was telling them, "As My loyal subjects, this is how you are to live." These words are not about how to get in or out of the kingdom. These words are about living within the kingdom under the gracious rule of Christ.

A certain rhythm marks the Christian life: the interplay between being forgiven and forgiving others. God forgives us through Christ. We forgive others. We receive and we give. Stubborn unforgiveness is incompatible with being a Christian. Remove forgiveness from the Christian life, and you've removed the very essence of what it means to be a Christian.

Our forgiveness and God's forgiveness are linked. His forgiveness empowers us to forgive others.

As Jesus expanded on the Fifth Petition right after the Lord's Prayer, later in His ministry, He gave a parable to enlarge the teaching even more. In Matthew 18, we read the parable of the unmerciful servant. Jesus told it after Peter tried to quantify the maximum number of times a person has to forgive. The parable answers that there is no maximum.

In the parable, a servant owed a king ten thousand talents, an astronomical debt (about twenty years' wages for a day laborer). The servant couldn't pay, so the king ordered the man and his family to be sold into slavery to pay his debt. The man begged for mercy. Feeling sorry, the king released the man and forgave the debt entirely.

The man went out and found a fellow servant who owed him a much lesser sum, a hundred denarii (about a hundred days' wages). The man began to choke the fellow servant, demanding payment. The fellow servant couldn't pay, so the man had him thrown into prison!

Do you see the absurdity in the story? To the king, it wasn't just absurd. It was outrageous! When the king heard about the unmerciful servant—how the king's grace had no effect on the man—the king reinstated the servant's debt and imprisoned him until he paid it in full.

You can probably guess how the story relates to us. God is the king. He has forgiven all our sins. We're the forgiven servant. And the people who sin against us are the fellow servants. When we hold grudges against others, we forget that God has forgiven us everything!

God wants us to forgive others! Really!

MISUNDERSTANDINGS ABOUT FORGIVENESS

Misunderstandings about forgiveness can cause significant anxiety for Christians. God expects us to forgive others, as He has forgiven us. You might worry, "Have I truly forgiven the other person? Is my attempt to forgive sufficient?" Unburden your conscience with the following distinctions:

Forgiving versus forgetting. Forgiving doesn't always mean forgetting. Although we'd like to erase painful memories, certain events become etched in our minds. In some cases, that's to our advantage. Think of the old saying—if a man cheats you once, shame on him; if he cheats you twice, shame on you.

Memory can protect us from making the same mistake twice. Remembering that someone hurt you can keep you from foolishly walking into the same trap again.

Forgiveness does not require forgetfulness. Memory still operates, even for those who show mercy.

Forgiveness versus reconciliation. Forgiveness requires one person. Reconciliation involves two. Ideally, two people come together and make amends, healing the relationship. A classic example is Jacob and Esau in Genesis 33. These two began fighting in the womb. As a young man, Jacob duped Esau out of a birthright, and later, Jacob stole the blessing from their father. Esau wanted to kill Jacob. Years passed, hearts softened, and when the two finally reunited, no one got hurt! They embraced and wept. That's reconciliation.

Many times, two people are not reconciled. One may be willing to make amends, while the other refuses.[37] Other times, one person may be inaccessible. Perhaps a son finally forgives a father long after the father's death.

In these cases, forgiveness doesn't heal a relationship. Instead, it heals *you.* Forgiveness frees your heart from bitterness and resentment.

---

37 See the case of Louis Zamperini and the Bird in chapter 14.

When possible, seek reconciliation. God, after all, "gave us the ministry of reconciliation" (2 Corinthians 5:18). When reconciliation isn't possible, be at peace, knowing that forgiveness frees you.

Difficulty versus unwillingness. Jesus' challenging words right after the Lord's Prayer really drive at this distinction. There's a difference between having a hard time forgiving someone and being unwilling to forgive. Sometimes it's hard to forgive. It can be a real struggle to move past painful experiences. You're trying, but it's hard. As Jeffrey Gibbs states in his commentary on Matthew's Gospel, "There will be times when all the disciple of Jesus can offer is a broken and a contrite heart: 'I know, Lord, what You require of me. I long to do it, but cannot, unless You help me.'"[38]

Unwillingness is the product of a hard heart, a stubborn will. Struggling to forgive is not the same as refusing to forgive. Refusing to forgive is turning your back on God's gift of grace, which, like a powerful current, flows through us to others. To shut off the flow is to shut off the stream at its source. Gibbs continues, "On the other hand, if a Christian looks another in the eye and says, 'I know what God requires of me, and I will not do it!' then that is a serious matter."[39]

You may struggle to forgive. Invite Jesus into the struggle with you, and rely on His strength when yours is not enough. He promises, "My grace is sufficient for you, for My power is made perfect in weakness" (2 Corinthians 12:9).

Ultimately, that's where it all ends up: reliance on God's grace. We need God's grace so that we can show others grace. By our own strength, moving beyond hurtful experiences can be near impossible. But God "is able to do far more abundantly than all we ask or think, according to the power at work within us" (Ephesians 3:20).

By His grace, He can help us to forgive.

---

38 Jeffrey A. Gibbs, *Matthew 1:1–11:1*, Concordia Commentary (St. Louis: Concordia Publishing House, 2006), 336.

39 Gibbs, *Matthew 1:1–11*, Concordia Commentary, 336.

FOR DISCUSSION

1. How did you learn the Lord's Prayer?

2. Were you surprised that the concluding doxology of the Lord's Prayer was almost certainly added later? Does that make it any less "holy"?

3. The chapter states, "Forgiving others is one of the most difficult demands of discipleship." Do you agree or disagree? Explain your answer.

4. In the parable of the unmerciful servant, put yourself in the place of the king. How would you have responded to the unmerciful servant after hearing about his cruel treatment of a fellow servant?

5. The unmerciful servant was shown extravagant grace but refused to extend any grace to his fellow servant. When do we, as forgiven children of God, find ourselves taking on the role of the unmerciful servant?

6. This chapter makes three distinctions: forgiving versus forgetting, forgiveness versus reconciliation, and difficulty versus unwillingness. Which of the three was most helpful to you? Why?

7. Read Genesis 33. What do you think moved Jacob and Esau to reconcile?

8. Jeffrey Gibbs modeled a prayer: "I know, Lord, what You require of me. I long to do it, but cannot, unless You help me." As a group, take time to pray for God to grant you a forgiving heart.

And the scribes who came down from Jerusalem were saying, "He is possessed by Beelzebul," and "by the prince of demons He casts out the demons." And He called them to Him and said to them in parables, "How can Satan cast out Satan? If a kingdom is divided against itself, that kingdom cannot stand. And if a house is divided against itself, that house will not be able to stand. And if Satan has risen up against himself and is divided, he cannot stand, but is coming to an end. But no one can enter a strong man's house and plunder his goods, unless he first binds the strong man. Then indeed he may plunder his house. **Truly, I say to you, all sins will be forgiven the children of man, and whatever blasphemies they utter, but whoever blasphemes against the Holy Spirit never has forgiveness, but is guilty of an eternal sin"**—for they were saying, "He has an unclean spirit."

MARK 3:22–30

An Unforgivable Sin?

An old story out of the Philippines involves a pastor and a woman in his congregation who claimed to speak with Jesus through dreams and visions.

The pastor was constantly guilt-ridden. He was haunted by regret over a secret sin he had committed years before.

The woman was constantly in demand. She was a phenomenon in the community. Day after day, people from all over the island stood at her doorway. They were waiting their turn to tell her their most pressing questions so that she could ask Jesus and relay the answer back to them.

The pastor was skeptical but decided to test the woman. What did he have to lose?

One day, he went to her house. One person in line recognized the pastor and invited him to the front of the line. The woman welcomed him into her home. Inside, he said to her, "Years ago, I did something terrible. I've never told anyone. Next time you talk to Jesus, ask Him what sin I committed. If He can tell you what the sin was, then I'll know you were really talking to Him."

Two weeks later, the woman visited the pastor at the church.

"Well, did you talk to Jesus?" he asked.

"I did," she said.

"Did you ask Him about my sin?"

"I did."

"Well, what did He say?" the pastor asked, ready to confirm that the woman was a fraud.

The woman responded, "I told Jesus, 'My pastor committed a sin that still burdens him. He wants to know if You know what it is.' Jesus looked at me and said, 'Ah, yes. Your pastor's sin. Hmm. I don't remember it anymore.'"

Nothing gives greater peace than knowing that God chooses to forget your sins. He says, "For I will be merciful toward their iniquities, and I will remember their sins no more" (Hebrews 8:12).

Through the cross and empty tomb, you've received a complete pardon.

But what if you couldn't be so certain about that? What if you committed an *unforgivable* sin?

In Mark 3:29, we read a terrifying combination of words: "eternal sin." Jesus announced a sin that God will not choose to forget. No forgiveness. No comfort.

Jesus' full statement is in Mark 3:28–29: "Truly, I say to you, all sins will be forgiven the children of man, and whatever blasphemies they utter, but whoever blasphemes against the Holy Spirit never has forgiveness, but is guilty of an eternal sin." Few statements have caused as much angst and desperate research as this one. The immediate reaction: An unforgivable sin? Have I committed it? Am I in danger of committing it?

A RESPONSE TO ACCUSATIONS

Jesus spoke these words in His hometown of Nazareth. A group of hostile scribes, or religious scholars, had come from Jerusalem to track Him down. They had an agenda. They wanted to discredit Jesus and derail His ministry.

In response to His exorcisms, they accused Jesus of being the devil's henchman. After all, they reasoned, how could He drive out Satan's agents without Satan's cooperation? Obviously, they underestimated Jesus' identity and power.

Jesus immediately exposed the absurdity of their allegations. "How can Satan cast out Satan?" Jesus asked them (Mark 3:23). Their assertion was completely illogical.

His opponents had it completely wrong. They said Jesus was possessed by an evil spirit when in fact, Jesus exhibited the power of the *Holy* Spirit. Jesus was fulfilling the words of Isaiah 42:1: "Behold My servant, whom I uphold, My chosen, in whom My soul delights; I have put My Spirit upon Him."

By their contemptuous speech, these men were blaspheming against the Holy Spirit. They maliciously misrepresented the Spirit of God, confusing it with the devil and His demons. Words have consequences, and none more severe than these spoken to Jesus.

WHAT IS THE UNFORGIVABLE SIN?

Understandings of the unforgivable sin are all over the map.

Some say it's willful rejection of Jesus. Others say the intent doesn't matter, only the words spoken.

Some say the eternal sin is a one-time offense—once committed, it's irreversible. Others say it's not a single moment but a lifetime of entrenched opposition to Christ.

Some say the unforgivable sin could only be committed when Jesus was walking on the earth, as a punishment for people who witnessed firsthand His miracles and attributed the miracles to the demonic power. Others say that people today can commit the unforgivable sin.

Martin Luther wrote that the sin against the Holy Spirit is "blaspheming His work and office, which brings, not God's command and wrath but pure grace and the forgiveness of all sins."[40]

Others contend that the sin is denying the person of Jesus as the Son of God.

One thing everyone can agree on: You want to avoid this sin at all costs!

From careful study of the text, some things are certain.

First, Jesus was responding to His opponents. He was not directly addressing His disciples, telling them not to slip into the unforgivable sin. He was not admonishing those who seek to follow Him and learn from His Word. He was addressing those who had set

---

40 *What Luther Says*, Ewald M. Plass, comp. (St. Louis: Concordia Publishing House, 1959), § 4244.

themselves firmly against Him and against the Holy Spirit's work through Him.

Second, blasphemy is an act of speech, not only of thought. Blasphemy is an outward expression of defiance against God. Jesus said in Matthew 10:32–33, "So everyone who acknowledges Me before men, I also will acknowledge before My Father who is in heaven, but whoever denies Me before men, I also will deny before My Father who is in heaven." Acknowledgment of Jesus is a result of faith. Denial of Jesus is a result of unbelief.

Along with Mark, the Gospels of Matthew and Luke also include Jesus' words about blasphemy against the Holy Spirit, the unforgivable sin. Matthew follows this teaching with additional words from Jesus that pinpoint the root of the problem—the heart. "Out of the abundance of the heart the mouth speaks" (Matthew 12:34).

Words reveal what's in a person's heart. Faith resides in the heart. In the same way, unbelief, the absence of faith, is a heart issue.

The passage teaches what the unforgivable sin is and what it's not. The unforgivable sin is ongoing rejection of Jesus, expressed outwardly through words that deny Jesus and His Spirit-empowered ministry. The unforgivable sin is not a threat hanging over the heads of believers.

THE TRUTH ABOUT FORGIVENESS

God wants us to find comfort in His gift of forgiveness. Think about it: If there is one unforgivable sin, that means every other sin is forgivable—and forgiven through Jesus!

If you, like the pastor in the opening story, are harboring memories of a secret sin, you can be certain that your sin is a not secret to God, who sees all things. Your sin is not a secret to Him, and He doesn't want His forgiveness to be a secret to you! Confess your sin to God, trust in His mercy, and find comfort in His gift of forgiveness.

Or maybe the sins that bother you aren't secret at all. Everyone knows about them. By foolish actions, you've brought shame upon yourself. By ill-advised decisions, you've damaged your reputation. You've fallen flat on your face, and everyone knows it.

God forgives those sins too.

Don't believe the lie that your sins are attached to you forever. By God's grace in Christ, they're not. God forgives you. By His cross and empty tomb, Jesus has erased your sins and overpowered the accuser, Satan.

It's important that we don't miss Jesus' point about the devil. In the text, the part about the unforgivable sin grabs our attention, and rightly so. But most of the passage is Jesus' response to the illogical accusation that He's working for the devil.

Right before referencing the eternal sin, Jesus made this key point: "No one can enter a strong man's house and plunder his goods, unless he first binds the strong man" (Mark 3:27). Jesus has done this for us. He has come to Satan's turf, this broken world, and He has overpowered the devil. "The prince of this world is judged" (John 16:11 KJV).

The devil wants to taunt you with your sin. He wants to cast doubt in your mind. He wants you to live in fear and insecurity about your eternal future. Jesus has outmuscled the strong man so that the devil's accusations would fall flat.

God's forgiveness through Jesus provides eternal comfort. His forgiveness completely covers your sins.

While this book was being written, my congregation was undergoing campus renovations with a building project, a new Family Life Center. For a time, the construction site was a conglomeration of rebar, tarp, pipes, dirt, and crushed rocks. It wasn't pristine looking, not at all.

Then came the day of the foundation pour. Cement trucks drove into the construction site one after another. Out of the trucks flowed cement, concealing all of the rebar, tarp, pipes, dirt, and crushed rocks. Once the pour was finished, you couldn't see what had been there. It was all covered over.

On the cross, Jesus poured out His blood for you and covers over your sins. Your guilt is no more.

WORDS THAT DELIGHT

Jesus warns against words that set people against Him in unbelief. But He delights in words that exude faith! A forgiven heart is a heart set free to praise God for His pardon! A heart cleansed by Christ is a heart filled with joy that must come forth in words! As Jesus said, "Out of the abundance of the heart the mouth speaks" (Matthew 12:34).

Or, as the prophet Jeremiah wrote, "If I say, 'I will not mention Him, or speak any more in His name,' there is in my heart as it were a burning fire shut up in my bones, and I am weary with holding it in, and I cannot" (20:9).

We'll end this chapter with words of praise. You might want to speak these out loud as a confession of faith!

The LORD is merciful and gracious,

slow to anger and abounding in steadfast love.

He will not always chide,

nor will He keep His anger forever.

He does not deal with us according to our sins,

nor repay us according to our iniquities.

For as high as the heavens are above the earth,

so great is His steadfast love toward those who fear Him;

as far as the east is from the west,

so far does He remove our transgressions from us.

PSALM 103:8–12

FOR DISCUSSION

1. Have you ever wondered about the unforgivable sin? How has this chapter added to your understanding?

2. The scribes accused Jesus of being demon-possessed. Why would Jesus' opponents make such an illogical accusation?

3. Do you believe that exorcisms of demons happen today? Explain your belief.

4. "Out of the abundance of the heart the mouth speaks" (Matthew 12:34). Think about words you've spoken today. What have those words revealed about your heart?

5. Why did Jesus call Satan "the prince of this world" (John 16:11 KJV)?

6. What kinds of accusations does Satan level at believers today?

7. Read more of Psalm 103. What words stand out to you? How do they represent your faith?

8. What would you say to someone who is worried about committing the unforgivable sin?

Challenging Words about OTHER TOPICS

You have heard that it was said, "You shall love your neighbor and hate your enemy." But I say to you, Love your enemies and pray for those who persecute you, so that you may be sons of your Father who is in heaven. For He makes His sun rise on the evil and on the good, and sends rain on the just and on the unjust. For if you love those who love you, what reward do you have? Do not even the tax collectors do the same? And if you greet only your brothers, what more are you doing than others? Do not even the Gentiles do the same? **You therefore must be perfect, as your heavenly Father is perfect.**

MATTHEW 5:43-48

Be Perfect?

t's not easy being a perfectionist. You might be one if...

- ❑ you struggle to accept being second-best at anything.
- ❑ you're afraid to fail and avoid activities when success isn't guaranteed.
- ❑ you're extremely critical of mistakes.
- ❑ you obsess over things that didn't go the way you wanted.
- ❑ you become defensive if someone points out deficiencies in your work.
- ❑ you feel crushed if you're not a top achiever.
- ❑ you procrastinate, afraid to start a project that may not end up perfect.
- ❑ you're an all-or-nothing thinker—"almost perfect" equals failure in your mind.

While the world benefits from people with high standards, perfectionism can be an oppressive burden. The guilt, the pressure, and the stress can be a lot to shoulder.

For those of us with perfectionist tendencies, it would be a relief to hear more words from Jesus like, "Come to Me, all who labor and are heavy laden, and I will give you rest" (Matthew 11:28). Those words are deeply refreshing, an invitation to entrust our cares to Jesus and find peace for our weary souls.

Jesus, the master Teacher, knows what we need to hear and gives us what we need. At times, we need words of grace to calm and reassure us. At other times, we need words of challenge to stir us from lethargy and refocus our priorities.

These must be the most challenging words ever spoken: "You therefore must be perfect, as your heavenly Father is perfect" (Matthew 5:48).

What an impossible task! To be perfect like God? Who can do that?

As a perfectionist, that's not what I want to hear from Jesus. I struggle trying to measure up to my own standards. How could I possibly measure up to God's?

HAVING THE RIGHT STANDARD

These words are part of Jesus' Sermon on the Mount. In His teachings, Jesus gave proper attention to both Law (what we do) and Gospel (what God does for us). The Sermon on the Mount is almost entirely Law. Jesus spoke these words to challenge.

In Matthew's Gospel, the Sermon on the Mount is Jesus' first major discourse. In the sermon, Jesus taught His disciples about what it means to follow Him. The sermon begins with the Beatitudes, statements of blessing. The remainder of the sermon shows how God's blessed children live in response to His grace, which has "delivered us from the domain of darkness and transferred us to the kingdom of His beloved Son, in whom we have redemption, the forgiveness of sins." (Colossians 1:13–14). The Sermon on the Mount teaches us how to think and conduct ourselves as disciples of Jesus.

One of the problems Jesus addresses in the sermon is the standard for Christian living. Is the standard people or God? The answer may seem obvious. God, of course, is the standard. But how often do we live as if people are the standard?

People have always compared themselves to one another, but today it seems like the comparison problem is amplified. We see the lives others project on social media and feel obligated to measure up to them. They're so smiley. I need to be happier. They're so accomplished. Why can't I accomplish more? They take such great vacations. I need to spend more and go more places.

I'll admit, I've had to fast from social media because my discontent with myself was growing, and it felt like every minute viewing others' posts only fed the monster within me.

When we evaluate ourselves against others, we're playing a losing game. Usually, we're comparing their strengths to our weaknesses. We're seeing a carefully selected slice of their life—the highlight reel—while we know the complete picture of our life, the good and the unfiltered bad.

If we fixate on others' lives and envy them, we've lost our focus. The focus shouldn't be *them*. It should be *Him*.

The comparison game existed in Jesus' time, even without social media! In first-century Jewish society, people admired the religious leaders and tried to emulate them. But Jesus said, "For I tell you, unless your righteousness exceeds that of the scribes and Pharisees, you will never enter the kingdom of heaven" (Matthew 5:20). If the scribes and Pharisees are your measuring stick, you're aiming too low!

Likewise, leading up to our key verse, Jesus tells His listeners to lift their sights higher: "For if you love those who love you, what reward do you have? Do not even the tax collectors do the same? And if you greet only your brothers, what more are you doing than others? Do not even the Gentiles do the same?" (Matthew 5:46–47).

In these verses from Matthew 5, Jesus was exposing the folly of comparing ourselves to people. On the one hand, if we're trying to become "high achievers" like the scribes and Pharisees, we're aiming for an unworthy target. On the other hand, if we're prideful and think we're outpacing everyone else, we may be shocked to discover we're no better than the "low achievers" like the tax collectors and Gentiles.

For a disciple of Jesus, human beings are inadequate standards for determining how to live. God is the only measurement that matters.

PERFECT?

The problem with having God as the standard is that He sets the bar impossibly high. Be perfect like God? We're all doomed to failure!

The Greek word for perfect is *teleios*. A better understanding of this word will help us grasp Jesus' point.

The word occurs nineteen times in the New Testament, though only three times in the Gospels. In some cases, English translations render it as "perfect." In other cases, it's translated as "mature," as in these verses:

> Brothers, do not be children in your thinking. Be infants in evil, but in your thinking be mature [*teleios*]. (1 Corinthians 14:20)

> But solid food is for the mature [*teleios*], for those who have their powers of discernment trained by constant practice to distinguish good from evil. (Hebrews 5:14)

In these cases, *teleios* is something achievable. By God's grace, we grow in maturity.

Even in cases where *teleios* is translated as "perfect," its meaning is different than what we might think. We think of perfect as flawless, without defects, passing inspection with a 100 percent rating. The biblical authors were less concerned with that kind of perfection—the kind over which we perfectionists obsess. Instead, the focus was more on being perfect in the sense of "complete, lacking in nothing" (James 1:4). In other words, when you're perfect, you have what you need in God's eyes. In this sense, perfect is not an unattainable ideal but a practical concept related to serving God as fully as possible.

Consider 1 John 4:18: "There is no fear in love, but perfect love casts out fear. For fear has to do with punishment, and whoever fears has not been perfected in love." John is not referring to reaching a state of sinlessness in this life. Unattainable for you and me! The greater concern is growing in faith and love toward others, empowered by God's perfect love dwelling in our hearts.

THE SAVIOR'S PERFECT WORK

The deeper you dig into the word *teleios*, the more treasures you uncover. *Teleios* is derived from a root word, *telos*.[41] *Telos* is a noun meaning "end" or "termination." Think of a telescope, which allows you to see the end of a great distance. *Telos* occurs forty-one times in the New Testament.

Teleios has multiple verb forms. One is *teleioo*, occurring twenty-three times in the New Testament. It refers to reaching completion. The word is used on multiple occasions to describe Jesus' work. If we only see the word through the lens of perfectionism, it can leave us scratching our heads. For example, Hebrews 5:9 says, "And being made perfect, He became the source of eternal salvation to all who obey Him."

How could Jesus be "made perfect"? Wasn't He already perfect?

In these verses, "perfect" describes what Jesus accomplished in real time. By fulfilling the prophecies and suffering for our sakes, He completed the work of salvation. You might say His résumé as Savior was made complete by His suffering and death.

Another verb form of *telos* is *teleo*, which occurs twenty-eight times in the New Testament. It means "to finish, fulfill, or accomplish." The verb *teleo* appears twice at the most crucial moment possible: as Jesus is dying on the cross. "After this, Jesus, knowing that all was now finished, said (to fulfill the Scripture), 'I thirst'" (John 19:28). His work had reached its goal. Jesus lived a flawless life. He fulfilled the Scriptures. He did it all with absolute perfection.

Two verses later, we read the culmination of Jesus' perfect work: "When Jesus had received the sour wine, He said, 'It is finished,' and He bowed His head and gave up His spirit" (John 19:30).

What was finished? Jesus' work of redemption for you and me. We do not live up to God's standards. We deserve punishment. Out of pure goodness and mercy, Jesus gave His life for us. On the cross, He fulfilled the purpose of His life on earth. He died as our Savior and would rise again in victory.

---

41 Danker, *A Greek-English Lexicon*, 998.

From these usages in John's crucifixion account, we see that *teleios* has to do with arriving at a destination, accomplishing a mission, reaching a goal. When Jesus tells us to be perfect as our Father is perfect, He's telling us that God is the goal. He's the destination. Our efforts find their end in Him alone.

OUR CONDUCTOR

None of us can reach God's level of perfection. That's why we count on the perfect work of Jesus on the cross to atone for our imperfection.

However, God still asks for perfection from us! He wants our faith to be mature and our love for others to be complete. He desires that we lack nothing in our calling as disciples of Jesus.

Jesus said, "Be perfect, as your heavenly Father is perfect." He also said, "Be merciful, even as your Father is merciful" (Luke 6:36). God is the standard!

I love the story of an orchestra player who was asked, "How do you keep from being discouraged when you get a negative review?" The negative review could come in the form of lackluster, half-hearted applause during the performance or a critical newspaper article the day afterward.

The performer answered, "I really don't pay attention to that. I'm only concerned with the feedback I get from my conductor. He's the one who knows what I'm supposed to be doing."

God is the standard. We measure ourselves against Him. He knows what we're supposed to be doing. His leadership of our lives is perfect in every sense of the word.

FOR DISCUSSION

1. Are you a perfectionist? How can you tell? (Don't stress about giving a perfect answer!)

2. What are the advantages and disadvantages of perfectionism?

3. Have you struggled with discontentment by comparing your life with others? How do you handle those feelings?

4. How are human standards and God's standards different from each other?

5. This chapter states, "When you're perfect, you have what you need in God's eyes." What do you need in God's eyes?

6. What does it mean to you to know that Jesus' work was finished (*teleo*) on the cross?

7. What can you learn from the orchestra player in the last part of this chapter?

8. Based on what you learned in this chapter, how can you strive to grow in spiritual maturity this week?

As they passed by in the morning, they saw the fig tree withered away to its roots. And Peter remembered and said to Him, "Rabbi, look! The fig tree that You cursed has withered." And Jesus answered them, "Have faith in God. Truly, I say to you, whoever says to this mountain, 'Be taken up and thrown into the sea,' and does not doubt in his heart, but believes that what he says will come to pass, it will be done for him. **Therefore I tell you, whatever you ask in prayer, believe that you have received it, and it will be yours.** And whenever you stand praying, forgive, if you have anything against anyone, so that your Father also who is in heaven may forgive you your trespasses."

MARK 11:20-25

Believe and Receive?

n 1943, Louis Zamperini agreed to a risky search-and-rescue mission over the Pacific Ocean. To his horror, while flying over the Pacific, two of the plane's four engines died, and the aircraft nosedived into the water. He and two companions floated on a life raft in the middle of the ocean for one week as sharks encircled them. A second week passed. In desperation, Louis did something he'd done only one other time in his life: he prayed. He had no church background, so he recited bits and pieces of prayers he'd heard in movies. Louis prayed that if God would spare his life, he'd dedicate his life to God. Louis survived after forty-seven days in the ocean. The Japanese picked him up and kept him as a prisoner of war for two years. He ended up being released and lived to age 97, dying in 2014.[42]

God can answer prayers in miraculous ways. Jesus said, "Whoever says to this mountain, 'Be taken up and thrown into the sea,' and does not doubt in his heart, but believes that what he says will come to pass, it will be done for him. Therefore I tell you, whatever you ask in prayer, believe that you have received it, and it will be yours" (Mark 11:23–24).

In Zamperini's case, rather than tossing a mountain into the sea, God preserved the life of a man lost at sea. His case is a dramatic one, and God would use it in a powerful way. I'll share more about that later.

---

42 Louis Zamperini's story is told compellingly in the book *Unbroken* by Laura Hillenbrand.

CAUSE AND EFFECT

There are two ways to understand what happened when Zamperini prayed. One is to think of it as cause and effect. He prayed, and as a result, God acted. We can apply this same understanding to Jesus' words. Tell the mountain to go into the sea, and God will do it. Believe what you ask for in prayer, and God will fulfill it. Cause and effect.

The problem is that the cause-and-effect understanding doesn't match up consistently with real life. Prayer is not always cause and effect. You can probably think of times in your life when you prayed for something and didn't get what you prayed for.

The disciples James and John found out firsthand that Jesus won't grant every request. One time, they asked, rather audaciously, for Jesus to give them prime seats in His eternal kingdom—one of them sitting at His right and one at His left. That's right—not Abraham or Moses, not David or Elijah, but James and John as cofavorites. They introduced their request by saying, "Teacher, we want You to do for us whatever we ask of You" (Mark 10:35).

They must have confused Jesus with the genie from Aladdin! You know the genie. He grants three wishes. He's bound to do whatever his master requests. Just say the word and—poof—your wish comes true!

Not so with Jesus. He told the ambitious brothers He couldn't fulfill their work order: "To sit at My right hand or at My left is not Mine to grant, but it is for those for whom it has been prepared" (Mark 10:40). A kinder rejection has never been given.

Through our prayers, we can't coerce God. We can't manipulate Him. We can't cause Him to veer from His divinely appointed plan.

We learn from personal experience that cause and effect is not a surefire formula for prayer. For His own perfect reasons, God doesn't always answer yes.

Sometimes He says, "My hour has not yet come" (John 2:4). The timing isn't right.

Sometimes He asks us to lean on Him more. Paul pleaded with the Lord to remove his thorn in the flesh, whatever that thorn may have been. God declined to remove the thorn but instead said to Paul, "My grace is sufficient for you, for My power is made perfect in weakness" (2 Corinthians 12:9). Rather than do exactly what we ask, God invites us to discover that His grace is sufficient for us.

REQUEST AND OUTCOME

Rather than cause and effect, a more realistic framework for understanding prayer is request and outcome. In prayer, we make a request. And what happens is the outcome. God, in His perfect wisdom, decides the outcome. You might pray for something, and the outcome is exactly as you asked. Other times, the outcome may be very different.

A request-and-outcome understanding of prayer curbs our unrealistic expectations. By accepting this framework, we humble ourselves under God's wisdom and sovereignty.

Do our prayers *influence* God? Absolutely! The Bible gives examples of people influencing God, even appearing to change His mind.

The stories of Abraham and Moses contain such instances. Abraham negotiated with God—successfully! When God was about to unleash His wrath on sinful Sodom, Abraham pleaded with God to spare the city for the sake of fifty righteous people. When God agreed to that, Abraham asked for mercy for forty-five. Then forty. Then thirty. Then twenty. Then ten. In response to Abraham's intercession, God delayed punishment.

Likewise, Moses pleaded with God to spare His own people, Israel. After the Israelites bowed down to a golden calf, God's divine anger was kindled. Moses appealed to God's promises to Abraham, Isaac, and Jacob. He held God to His word. God is always true to His word. And so the people were spared.

Abraham and Moses influenced God. But they did not control God by their prayers. There's a difference. The outcome ultimately was God's choice.

INGREDIENTS OF PRAYER

A request-and-outcome framework helps us interpret Jesus' teaching on prayer. As far as I know, no human has ever successfully relocated a mountain into the sea by believing it would happen. If we fixate on the mountain imagery, we miss the point. The point is faith. Immediately before the mountain verse, Jesus said, "Have faith in God" (Mark 11:22). In each of the next two sentences, Jesus said, "Believe." Jesus' words are a teaching on faith. He wants us to have a strong, unshakable, ridiculously confident faith in God. He wants us to believe so firmly in an all-powerful God that we wouldn't be surprised if He tossed a mountain into the sea.

This teaching falls under the category of hyperbole. Hyperbole uses an impossible illustration to make an unforgettable point. Hyperbole is not to be taken literally. It is meant to be taken seriously.

Context reveals why Jesus chose the image of a mountain to make His point. A few verses before in Mark 11, Jesus had just cursed a fig tree. The disciples were marveling at His power. They were at the Mount of Olives. In His words on prayer, Jesus referred not just to a mountain. He spoke of "this mountain." Picture Him motioning to the mountainside around them and saying, "If you were impressed by what happened to this tree, God can do even greater things with this mountain. Believe in God with all of your heart."

In the text, Jesus teaches us about two essential ingredients for God-honoring prayers. These two ingredients describe the heart that God desires in all who pray to Him.

The first ingredient is faith. God desires a believing heart. As James wrote, "But let him ask in faith, with no doubting, for the one who doubts is like a wave of the sea that is driven and tossed by the wind" (1:6). Faith anchors our requests to God's goodness, appealing on the basis of His unlimited mercy.

The second ingredient comes in the next verse: "And whenever you stand praying, forgive, if you have anything against anyone, so that your Father also who is in heaven may forgive you your trespasses"

(Mark 11:25). Jesus tells us to pray with faith and forgiveness. He desires a trusting heart and a softened heart.

Faith and forgiveness go hand in hand. If you and I are holding on to bitterness, if we're refusing to let go of a grudge, if unforgiveness is darkening our hearts, then we're out of sync with God. As Lutheran commentator R. C. H. Lenski wrote, "It is most vital for acceptable prayer that the petitioner forgive all his fellow men. Let us not delude ourselves that we are most firmly believing and filling our prayers with faith, while secretly our hearts hold something against somebody."[43]

A SOFTENED HEART

Jesus spoke of God moving mountains. Let me tell you about the biggest mountain that God ever moved. It was the mountain of sin that divided us from Him. On the Mount of Olives, Jesus agonized over the pain that awaited Him. On Mount Calvary, He suffered on the cross, dying for our sakes. He removed the mountain of sins that you and I compile through our thoughts, words, and actions. He hurled that mountain into the sea so that our sins are no more.

When we have faith and forgiveness in our hearts, then we're approaching God the way He wants to be approached. He desires a trusting heart, holding on to His goodness and promises. He desires a softened heart, a heart that gives and receives grace. God does not consider the content of our prayers apart from the condition of our hearts.

Forgiveness was an important part of Zamperini's story. While in the Japanese prisoner-of-war camp for two years, he endured horrifyingly inhumane treatment. Chief among his tormentors was a prison guard nicknamed "the Bird," who sadistically targeted Zamperini day after day. After being freed, Zamperini's life back in the United States was a mess. He spiraled downward, unable to recover from the trauma he experienced. One day, he attended an evangelistic rally, where he heard the Gospel. Slowly, God's Word took root in Zamperini's life, and he was a changed man.

---

43 Lenski, *The Interpretation of St. Mark's and St. Luke's Gospels*, 312.

The biggest change was the desire to forgive. While in Japan for the Winter Olympics in 1998, after extensive searching, Zamperini established contact with his former tormentor, the Bird, then an old man. Zamperini asked for a meeting so that he could personally forgive the Bird. The Bird refused to see him. Accepting that he'd never get to forgive his tormentor face-to-face, Zamperini sent a letter to the Bird. Zamperini had overcome his own bitterness with God's help. He was no longer a prisoner of war nor a prisoner of anger. He was truly a free man.

Jesus teaches us to approach God with faith and forgiveness in our hearts. You can't control what happens after you pray. The outcome is in God's hands. But you can determine what goes into your prayers. With the Holy Spirit's help, you can pray with confident faith. By the grace of Christ, you can pray with a heart set free by forgiveness.

With prayers marked by faith and forgiveness, you're approaching God the way He wants to be approached. We can be confident that God will respond according to His will, and we know His will is the very best for us.

FOR DISCUSSION

1. What do you think it was like to float for forty-seven days in the ocean?

2. What's your reaction to the cause-and-effect and request-and-outcome paradigms? Do you agree or disagree with the author's comparison of these two concepts?

3. Have you struggled with God's timing in answering your prayers? Share an example.

4. Have you been able to look back in hindsight and see God's wisdom in how a prayer was answered? Share what happened.

5. God listened to the pleas of Abraham and Moses and spared sinful people. What do these examples teach us about God's mercy?

6. Why does Jesus say forgiveness is an essential ingredient for prayer?

7. Using your imagination, what do you suppose Louis Zamperini wrote in his letter to the Bird?

8. To some extent, we all want to be in control. However, as the chapter states, "You can't control what happens after you pray. The outcome is in God's hands." How does this lack of control make you feel?

[Jesus] arose and went away to the region of Tyre and Sidon. And He entered a house and did not want anyone to know, yet He could not be hidden. But immediately a woman whose little daughter had an unclean spirit heard of Him and came and fell down at His feet. Now the woman was a Gentile, a Syrophoenician by birth. And she begged Him to cast the demon out of her daughter. And **He said to her, "Let the children be fed first, for it is not right to take the children's bread and throw it to the dogs."** But she answered Him, "Yes, Lord; yet even the dogs under the table eat the children's crumbs." And He said to her, "For this statement you may go your way; the demon has left your daughter." And she went home and found the child lying in bed and the demon gone.

MARK 7:24-30

Did Jesus Call a Woman a Dog?

Are you a dog person? In my family, we're dog people. Growing up, we always had one or two dogs. Dogs are great. They're always happy to see you. They're excellent listeners. They perceive distress and provide comfort. And they're better than vacuum cleaners under the dinner table. In our culture, dogs are beloved household pets.

Not so in Bible times. In those days, dogs were mostly scavengers. Wild dogs devoured Queen Jezebel after she fell to her death. King David described his enemies this way: "Each evening they come back, howling like dogs and prowling about the city" (Psalm 59:6). Paul was not admiring the canine species when he wrote, "Look out for the dogs, look out for the evildoers" (Philippians 3:2).

In His words recorded in Mark 7:27, Jesus was not complimenting a woman who interrupted His quiet time with a desperate need. Jesus had retreated to Gentile territory. His popularity was soaring among His fellow Jews. Crowds were overwhelming Him everywhere He went. His opponents were challenging Him constantly. He longed for peace and solitude. Mark 7:24 says, "And He entered a house and did not want anyone to know, yet He could not be hidden."

No, He couldn't. No sooner had the door closed behind Him than a woman burst into the house. Wide-eyed. Out of breath. Frantic. She fell at Jesus' feet. She began begging Him to heal her demon-possessed daughter.

What nerve! The woman had no credentials to approach Jesus. We're told she was a Gentile, "a Syrophoenician by birth" (Mark 7:26). As a Gentile, a religious and cultural outsider, a woman in a male-dominated society, a mother of an unclean daughter, and now an uninvited guest, she checked the wrong box in every category. Still, she came boldly asking Jesus to cast out the demon. Jesus responded in Mark 7:27: "Let the children be fed first, for it is not right to take the children's bread and throw it to the dogs."

Did He just call the woman a dog? You'd expect that Jesus would be above name-calling. In our culture of put-downs, demeaning comments, and harsh labels, we want to open the Bible and find a Savior who rises above pettiness. But here, we find Jesus equating the woman with a dog. Some will point out that in the original Greek, Jesus uses a diminutive form of the word *dog*, more like *puppy*, softening the blow. Nonetheless, in any culture, a dog is always below a human, and it especially was in the culture of Jesus' day.

From this story, two disturbing questions demand to be addressed. Is Jesus sexist? And is He racist? At first glance, it appears that Jesus was talking down to the woman either because she was a woman or a Gentile or both. Could it be?

IS JESUS SEXIST?

In the Gospels, we see that Jesus valued women in many ways.[44]

With deep compassion, Jesus healed women. He cured Peter's mother-in-law of a fever. A woman who had been bleeding for years touched His robe and was cured; He even turned around and spoke to her, an unexpected act of compassion. He laid His hands on a woman who was bent over, and at His touch, she straightened up. Jesus brought back to life a twelve-year-old girl, Jairus's daughter. Our Lord also noticed a grieving mother in a funeral procession; He interrupted the procession to restore her son's life.

Jesus highlighted women as models of faith. He commended a poor widow for giving all she had in the offering plate. He taught

---

44 Because there are so many examples in quick succession, for ease of reading, Scripture references for the following stories are included in the Scripture References appendix.

about a persistent widow as a model of prayer and persistence. He featured five wise virgins as examples of preparedness.

Jesus defended women by teaching against lust and divorce.

To women with scandalous backgrounds, Jesus showed respect and mercy. He protected a woman caught in adultery when her accusers attempted to stone her. At a well, He conversed respect-fully with a woman who had been married five times. He cast seven demons out of a woman who then became an unwavering follower: Mary Magdalene.

Jesus honored His mother, Mary. He performed His first miracle at her request. While hanging on the cross, Jesus entrusted His mother to His best friend, John.

Jesus cried with Mary and Martha. Then He raised their brother, Lazarus, back to life.

After rising from the grave, He honored His female followers by making them the first witnesses of the resurrection.

As you can see, Jesus had an extensive track record of love and respect for women.

IS JESUS RACIST?

To the Syrophoenician woman, Jesus said, "I was sent only to the lost sheep of the house of Israel" (Matthew 15:24). Though He was sent to the lost sheep of Israel, His love was big enough to encompass all of humankind. He said, "And I have other sheep that are not of this fold. I must bring them also, and they will listen to My voice" (John 10:16). Jesus' sheep includes everyone, both Jews and Gentiles (that is, anyone who is not a Jew).

The first Gentiles to meet Him were the Magi (Matthew 2:1–12).

In Jesus' public ministry, His first Gentile encounter recorded in the Gospels is with a Roman centurion. With no hint of prejudice, Jesus healed the man's servant and remarked, "I tell you, not even in Israel have I found such faith" (Luke 7:9).

In one of the few instances when Jesus traveled outside of His native land, He went to the other side of the Sea of Galilee, to a region called the Gerasenes. There, He encountered a demon-possessed man. Jesus cast the demons into a herd of pigs, which then went squealing off a cliff into the sea. Showing His love for the man and those of his race, Jesus said to him, "Go home to your friends and tell them how much the Lord has done for you, and how He has had mercy on you" (Mark 5:19).

He healed a deaf man in the Gentile region of the Decapolis (Mark 7:31–37).

After His resurrection, Jesus gave the Great Commission to make disciples of all nations (Matthew 28:19). Before His ascension, Jesus said to His disciples, "You will be My witnesses in Jerusalem and in all Judea and Samaria, and to the end of the earth" (Acts 1:8).

Jesus is the Creator of every race and the Redeemer of all humanity. Throughout His earthly ministry, He was filled with love for all people.

PERCEIVING THE PARABLE

To understand Jesus' words, we need to approach His statement as a parable—an earthly story with a heavenly meaning. To the woman, Jesus spoke a parable about His priorities. When Jesus told her that He was sent only to the lost sheep of Israel, He was speaking about sequence. He was not suggesting an inherent superiority of one group over another. The mission to all nations would come, but not yet. Strategic outreach to Gentiles would commence after His ascension on Pentecost and throughout the Book of Acts.

For now, the woman would have to accept her assigned lot. "Let the children be fed first, for it is not right to take the children's bread and throw it to the dogs." Those may sound like tough words. But the woman was perceptive. She picked up on Jesus' tactic in this parabolic speech.

Without missing a beat, the woman responded to Jesus *from within the parable*. She answered cleverly in Mark 7:28, "Yes, Lord; yet even the dogs under the table eat the children's crumbs." She wasn't asking for the children's food—just for the crumbs. She wasn't requesting to eat before the children, but she also refused to wait. Crumbs fall to the ground while children eat. My dogs didn't wait until after the meal. They were right there, ready to catch the crumbs before they hit the ground!

The woman perceived that a crumb of grace from Jesus would be plenty. What a great lesson of faith! Just a crumb of grace from Jesus will meet your needs. He's the God who commends mustard-seed faith, the God who empowered a little boy to defeat a giant, the God who comes to us in a tiny piece of bread and a tiny drop of wine. A little from Jesus is more than enough for us.

Jesus has more than enough grace for you and me today. His grace is ours because of what He suffered in our place. He humbled Himself. He subjected Himself to those who would tear His flesh. As Psalm 22:16 says about Him, "For dogs encompass Me; a company of evildoers encircles Me; they have pierced My hands and feet." Jesus became lower than the dogs. Through His sacrifice on the cross, you and I find a place at His table as sons and daughters of God. A crumb from Him is more than enough. And He gives us so much more than a crumb. He gives us heaven and every spiritual blessing.

HUMILITY AND PERSISTENCE

Jesus' grace is enough for you and me and enough for the woman. After her response, Jesus said in Mark 7:29, "For this statement you may go your way; the demon has left your daughter." Jesus was looking for genuine faith in the woman. He was looking for a heart that would not take offense but would accept whatever He chose to give her. He found that kind of faith, a faith marked by humility and persistence.

The woman was humble. So often, we assert ourselves based on our perceived rights. With an illusion of our own goodness, we may feel that we deserve something or that we're entitled to something. Not this woman. She accepted Jesus' terms. He owed her nothing; she knew that. She appealed to Him not based on her rights but based on His goodness. She had a humble faith.

And she had a persistent faith. She refused to give up. She was that determined type of person known as . . . a mom. Moms and dads will stop at nothing to protect their children. Her daughter was sick. The woman wouldn't take no for an answer. One time, Jesus told a parable about a widow and an unjust judge. The lesson of that story, according to Luke 18:1, is "always to pray and not lose heart."

The Syrophoenician woman was persistent. She was a desperate mom, anxious to save her daughter. After Jesus, she had no plan B. He was her one and only hope.

Jesus is our one and only hope too. We have no plan B. Jesus is it. And His grace is more than enough for us. A crumb from His table is worth more than a feast anywhere else. Jesus was looking for a faith marked by humility and persistence in the woman, and He looks for the same from us.

Jesus is looking for humble faith. We're often disappointed because we're not getting what we feel we deserve from God. He owes us nothing. Everything is a gift. And He loves to give blessing upon blessing to us. By faith, we accept His gifts with thanksgiving.

Jesus is looking for persistent faith. In prayer, we practice persistence. We have no plan B. The Bible presents no alternative to Jesus. In all your needs, don't be discouraged. Keep coming back to Him. Be persistent in prayer. God honors unyielding faith in Him.

Jesus is looking for faith marked by humility and persistence. In humility, we live our lives on His terms, not our own. With persistence, we never stop seeking Him in all our needs. A crumb from Jesus is more than enough. Yet He does better than that. Through His immeasurable grace for us, He tells us to pull up a chair at the table. That's where His children belong.

FOR DISCUSSION

1. Are you a dog person, a cat person, or neither? Explain your affinity (or lack thereof).

2. What did you observe from this chapter about Jesus' interactions with women?

3. What did you notice about Jesus' interactions with Gentiles?

4. What can you learn from the Syrophoenician woman's boldness? In what area of life could you benefit from more assertiveness?

5. This chapter states, "Jesus was looking for a faith marked by humility and persistence in the woman, and He looks for the same from us." What are barriers to humility? How do we overcome those obstacles?

6. What are barriers to persistence? How do we overcome those obstacles?

7. Read Matthew 7:7–11. What is Jesus saying about boldness in our faith?

8. If you were to approach Jesus with a bold request, what would it be? Dedicate prayer time to present your request boldly!

"Let not your hearts be troubled. Believe in God; believe also in Me. In My Father's house are many rooms. If it were not so, would I have told you that I go to prepare a place for you? And if I go and prepare a place for you, I will come again and will take you to Myself, that where I am you may be also. And you know the way to where I am going." Thomas said to Him, "Lord, we do not know where You are going. How can we know the way?" **Jesus said to him, "I am the way, and the truth, and the life. No one comes to the Father except through Me.** If you had known Me, you would have known My Father also. From now on you do know Him and have seen Him."

JOHN 14:1-7

Only One Way to God?

A couple of weeks ago, my wife and I took our children to a pumpkin patch with a hay maze. The children enjoyed trying to find their way through the walls of bundled hay. From our vantage point as adults, we could see over the top and had a clear view of the dead-ends and the way out. The children, being shorter, had to work through the maze one step at a time, navigating turns, sometimes backtracking. Eventually, they emerged from the exit triumphant, having conquered the maze!

It seems simple enough: For the maze, there was one way in and one way out. For something like a maze, no one challenges the one-way arrangement. For something much more profound than a bunch of hay, however, the one-way argument strikes some as offensive and unfair.

In John 14:6, Jesus said, "I am the way, and the truth, and the life. No one comes to the Father except through Me." Jesus' words here are consistent with other statements He made. In John 10:7, Jesus said, "I am the door of the sheep." Other New Testament writings reinforce Jesus' claim. In Ephesians 2:18, Paul writes that through Christ, we "have access in one Spirit to the Father."

In many places, the Bible teaches Jesus as the way to the Father and eternal life.

A pastor (whose theological views differ from mine on several points) wrote about a time he attended a funeral led by a young preacher. At the service, the preacher was reading the opening verses of John 14, which include, "In My Father's house are many rooms. If it were not so, would I have told you that I go to prepare a place for you?" (v. 2). The opening verses of John 14 are comforting words that declare our eternal hope in Christ.

The observing pastor reveled in the majestic beginning of verse 6: "I am the way, and the truth, and the life." Then he wondered if the young preacher would stop the reading there or finish the verse. When the preacher read the second half of verse 6—"No one comes to the Father except through Me"—the observing pastor said the man next to him expressed offense at those last words. The man muttered that the preacher was, right there in the sermon, condemning all the non-Christians in the room.

Some people hear Jesus' words in that way, as condemnation. It's unfortunate that Jesus' words come across that way to some. Jesus Himself stated elsewhere, "For God did not send His Son into the world to condemn the world, but in order that the world might be saved through Him" (John 3:17). Jesus' purpose is salvation, not condemnation.

For some people, Jesus' claim strikes them as unfair. For those who hold such a view, certain biblical truths appear to be at odds. God "desires all people to be saved" (1 Timothy 2:4), and yet none will be saved apart from Christ. How do we reconcile God's desire for all to be saved with the reality that God's revealed method of salvation is faith in Christ alone?

UNDERSTANDING THE DILEMMA

Before exploring some implications of Jesus' claim in John 14:6, let me share some preliminary thoughts.

First, if we're repulsed by Jesus' claim, we're making a false assumption. Humanity did not enjoy open access to God before Christ. God didn't suddenly change the rules and limit salvation only to Christ-followers. In actuality, because of our sinful condition, none of us deserve salvation. When Jesus announced Himself as the way to the Father, He was not shrinking the path of salvation. He was opening the door to heaven. Without Christ, the number of saved is zero. With Christ, "everyone who calls on the name of the Lord will be saved" (Romans 10:13).

Second, Jesus is not speaking words of rejection in John 14:6. These are words of *invitation*. He's inviting all to trust in Him and find life in Him.

Third, if you feel troubled by the thought that some will not enter eternal life, that's an appropriate feeling. You and I *should* be bothered by the idea that some people will spend eternity apart from God.

In Matthew 25, Jesus described a division of all humanity into sheep and goats. To the sheep, He'll say joyfully, "Come, you who are blessed by My Father, inherit the kingdom prepared for you from the foundation of the world" (Matthew 25:34). To the goats, He'll say, with sadness, "Depart from Me, you cursed, into the eternal fire prepared for the devil and his angels" (Matthew 25:41).

Eternal punishment was not created for people. It was prepared for the devil and his angels. It's not God's will for any human to spend eternity apart from Him, which is the very definition of hell. If the concept of eternal torment bothers you, it *should*. It bothers God too. It bothers Him so much that He sent His Son to suffer the torment of the cross, where He cried out, "My God, My God, why have You forsaken Me?" (Matthew 27:46).

If you and I were not affected by the thought of people spending eternity apart from God, we'd be calloused and heartless. Thinking, "It shouldn't be this way," regarding hell is a holy, righteous indignation. But we should aim our indignation not at Jesus but at His opponents—the devil and his evil angels—who desperately want company in their eternal sufferings and are determined to lead people away from Jesus.

QUESTIONS

Here are some questions that relate to Jesus' words in John 14:6. The responses are not exhaustive but will give you a framework for thinking about these theological issues.

"What about those who have never heard of Jesus?"

This is a real struggle!

Around the world, countless people have not heard of Jesus—at least, as far as we know. It's possible for Jesus to appear personally to unbelievers, as He appeared on the road to Damascus to Saul (who became Paul). Some Christian church bodies, either formally or informally, hold to an idea of "anonymous Christians." The concept rests on speculation, assuming that some people who are ignorant of the Gospel would respond with faith if they had heard it. Based on that inclination of the heart, God grants them salvation.

A concern for those who have not heard motivates evangelism and mission work. Every day, brave missionaries build relationships within foreign people groups and share the Gospel. Your prayers and financial support of missionaries can make an eternal impact on those who hear the Good News!

In some ways, it would be easy to argue that this question is none of our business. It's not our business to decide who goes to heaven and who goes to hell. Only God can judge. Rather than invest our time in trying to answer this question, we can spend that time using whatever gifts God has given us to share the Good News of salvation with our words and in our lives. Best of all, we can pray for all people to be saved. We can pray for those who have never heard about Jesus.

I hold out hope that people who have never heard of Jesus will hear about Him and believe in Him for eternal life!

"What about committed adherents of other religions?"

This, too, is a real struggle!

You may know people of other religions who are kind, generous, ethical, and loving. They may outpace most Christians in good deeds. Their religion directs their actions and leads them to live a "good life." People of all religions make valuable contributions to society.

The sticky point is that according to Scripture, salvation is by grace, not by works. God's grace is ours by faith in Christ. No matter how good of a life someone lives—Christian or non-Christian—it's not enough to merit eternity. "For all have sinned and fall short of the glory of God, and are justified by His grace as a gift, through the redemption that is in Christ Jesus" (Romans 3:23–24).

As for how Christians can claim to stand apart from all other religions, the playing field isn't as wide as you may think. For many years, I've benefitted from the teaching of Dr. Francis Pieper, whose almost-a-century-old *Christian Dogmatics* textbooks are still required reading at the seminary I attended. In the opening pages of his first volume, Pieper asserts that there are not thousands of religions in the world but "only two essentially different religions: the religion of the Law, that is, the endeavor to reconcile God through man's own works, and the religion of the Gospel, that is, faith in the Lord Jesus Christ, belief wrought through the Gospel by the Holy Ghost that we have a gracious God through the reconciliation already effected by Christ, and not because of our own works."[45]

Pieper reduces all world religions to two: works and grace. Christianity uniquely is the religion of grace. Only in Christianity does God step into history and personally perform the work needed for our salvation. All other religions place the burden on the individual to perform. In Christianity, God comes down to us. All other religions expect you to work your way up. Christianity alone points to the completed work of God's Son.

How do we then approach people of other religions? Peter offered these words: "But in your hearts honor Christ the Lord as holy, always being prepared to make a defense to anyone who asks you for a reason for the hope that is in you; yet do it with gentleness and respect" (1 Peter 3:15). That verse is packed with meaning!

First, be prepared. It's hard to predict when an opportunity to share your faith might arise. Have a solid understanding of your beliefs so that you can articulate your faith clearly, trusting the Holy Spirit to guide you. We equip ourselves by studying Scripture and praying.

Second, be a person of hope. If you're always gloomy, no one wants to share in that. In Titus 2:10, Paul instructs Titus to "make the teaching about God our Savior attractive" (NIV). A hopeful attitude attracts and intrigues.

---

45 Francis Pieper, *Christian Dogmatics*, vol. 1 (St. Louis: Concordia Publishing House, 1950), 10.

Third, do it with gentleness and respect. Arrogance is a huge turn-off! Gentle outperforms pushy any day. Respectful works better than presumptuous. Sharing the right information in the wrong manner is counterproductive. Leading people into a relationship with Jesus happens through caring relationships.

"What about Old Testament believers?"

More a point of curiosity than a pressing dilemma, some have wondered how Old Testament believers could be saved since Jesus had not yet been born, and therefore they could not yet know Him as the way, the truth, and the life.

Jesus said to the disciple Thomas, "Blessed are those who have not seen and yet have believed" (John 20:29). These words apply to you and me. We haven't seen Jesus with our eyes, yet we believe and are blessed through faith. Similarly, the Old Testament faithful didn't see Jesus with their eyes, but they had faith in God and His promise of a Savior. We look backward in history to the cross. They looked forward to His coming. The cross stands at the center of history as the hope of those who lived before and after Jesus' first coming.

Abraham was commended for his faith. And not just faith in a vague concept of a divine being but faith in the Father and in the Savior He would send. Jesus said, "Your father Abraham rejoiced that he would see My day. He saw it and was glad" (John 8:56). Scripture regards Abraham as the father of faith. He is commended not because he could foresee all the details of Jesus as a person but because he trusted in God as his Savior and found comfort in God's promises. "Those who are of faith are blessed along with Abraham, the man of faith" (Galatians 3:9).

Moses and Elijah are two more examples of God's saving plan for Old Testament believers. At Jesus' transfiguration, Moses and Elijah appeared with Jesus and spoke to Him about His impending departure. These two giants of the Old Testament were already in the perfect presence of God and were face-to-face with their Savior at that moment.

God, who never changes, doesn't distinguish between believers who lived before Jesus' earthly life and those who lived after, like you and me. As the Bible's great chapter on faith says, "Now faith is the assurance of things hoped for, the conviction of things not seen. For by it the people of old received their commendation" (Hebrews 11:1–2). The words "people of old" are a direct reference to the people of the Old Testament, and we are clearly told they received their commendation by faith.

THE NARROW GATE

Jesus said, "Enter by the narrow gate. For the gate is wide and the way is easy that leads to destruction, and those who enter by it are many. For the gate is narrow and the way is hard that leads to life, and those who find it are few" (Matthew 7:13–14).

Many people prefer to think of salvation as a wide gate. I recall a friendly debate with a pastor of another denomination who subscribed to the wide-gate theory. He believed that all religious viewpoints are equally valid and all paths lead to God.

I suggested his theology was inherently contradictory. You can't in one breath say all religious viewpoints are valid and then in the next breath say my viewpoint is invalid because I believe that Jesus is the only way to God. If all viewpoints are valid, mine has to be too. And if mine is, then the others aren't.

Jesus said the gate is narrow, but He doesn't say it's limited. Heaven has no maximum capacity. God's grace has no limit. The gate may be narrow, but God desires for every human being to enter through it. He has room for all. Remember, a few sentences before His statement about being the way, the truth, and the life, Jesus said, "In My Father's house are many rooms" (John 14:2). Many rooms! Innumerable rooms! God has space for all who trust in His only Son as their Savior.

This is good news! This is *the* Good News! God loves us so much that He gives us Jesus as our Savior!

Tell someone!

FOR DISCUSSION

1. This chapter referenced a person who took offense to this Bible verse at a funeral: "No one comes to the Father except through Me" (John 14:6). What was the man's objection? What's your reaction to his reaction?

2. How would you answer this question posed in the chapter: What about those who have never heard of Jesus?

3. How about this one: What about committed adherents of other religions?

4. How do you feel about the suggestion that all world religions fall under one of two categories—a religion of works and a religion of grace? Do you agree or disagree with that way of categorizing religions?

5. Read 1 Peter 3:15. What is this verse saying to you?

6. What prevents us from telling others about Jesus?

7. Tell about a time when you told someone about Jesus. What was the result?

8. Whose salvation can you pray for today?

Conclusion

One time, before predicting His death, Jesus said to His disciples, "Let these words sink into your ears" (Luke 9:44).

Jesus wants His words to sink in. He didn't speak words that would make a slight impression and then fade. His words weren't designed to give a momentary feeling or spark a fleeting thought. He spoke words that, by the Holy Spirit's power, take root in human hearts and change lives.

What are we to do with Jesus' words, including His most challenging teachings? In the concluding teaching of the Sermon on the Mount, Jesus said, "Everyone then who hears these words of Mine and does them will be like a wise man who built his house on the rock" (Matthew 7:24). The house on the rock is sturdy. It withstands storms. Jesus and His words have that kind of strength.

Notice that Jesus spoke of hearing and *doing* His words. It's not enough simply to hear. His words are transformative, changing the way we live.

Hearing and doing involves believing what He says, letting it sink in, and living differently because His words have changed you. Hearing and doing is putting God first, loving your family, honoring marriage, being a responsible steward, speaking kindly, forgiving, sharing your faith, and much more. Through the power of the Holy Spirit, Jesus' words shape our lives so that we live more fully for God's glory.

The Teacher's lessons are timeless—for people of His day, people today, and future generations. "Heaven and earth will pass away, but My words will not pass away" (Luke 21:33).

Jesus' teachings endure.

Scripture References

This section is a resource to take you deeper into God's Word. On the following pages, you'll find a quick reference of Bible verses used in each chapter. None of these verses occur in isolation; all are part of a larger argument or narrative contained in Scripture. I encourage you to read these verses in your Bible and notice the context around them. With thoughtful consideration of God's Word and guided by the Holy Spirit, you can confidently participate in conversations about the topics addressed in this book.

CHAPTER 1: "A TEACHER COME FROM GOD"

Key text: John 3:2

Jesus knew what was in man: John 2:25

Jesus as Teacher: Mark 10:17; Luke 12:13; 19:39; 20:39; John 11:28

Jesus as Teacher and Lord: John 13:13

Jesus as Prophet: Matthew 21:11; Deuteronomy 18:15–18; Hebrews 1:1–2

Kingdom of God as Jesus' overarching theme: Matthew 4:17; 6:10; 6:33; 7:21; 7:28; 12:28; 16:28

Examples of teaching techniques: proverbs (Matthew 7:12); questions (Matthew 22:20); parables (Luke 10:25–37; 15:11–32); overstatement (Mark 9:43); and hyperbole (Mark 10:25)

God's Word is living and active: Hebrews 4:12

Jesus as fulfiller of the Old Testament: Matthew 5:17

CHAPTER 2: HATE MY FAMILY?

Key text: Luke 14:25–30, 33
God is love: 1 John 4:8
Loving Jesus the most: Matthew 10:37
God above all else: Exodus 20:3
Trying to serve two masters: Matthew 6:24
Obeying God rather than men: Acts 5:29
Jesus in His Father's house: Luke 2:48–49; 2:51
Honor father and mother: Exodus 20:12
Straining toward what is ahead: Philippians 3:13
Abraham and Isaac: Genesis 22:12
The Lamb who was slain: Revelation 5:12
The surpassing greatness of knowing Christ:
    Philippians 3:7–8
Love God with all your mind: Luke 10:27
Fruit of the Spirit: Galatians 5:22

CHAPTER 3: NOT PEACE BUT A SWORD?

Key text: Matthew 10:32–39
Christ as bringer of peace: Isaiah 9:6; Luke 2:14
The Sermon on the Mount: Matthew 5–7
Jesus' Missionary Discourse: Matthew 10
Instructions for wives and husbands, children and parents:
    Ephesians 5–6
As for me and my house: Joshua 24:15
Put away your sword: Matthew 26:52
Division over Christ among the crowds: John 7:12; 7:43–44
Calling disciples to leave family: Mark 1:17, 20
Righteous through faith: Romans 3:22
Sheep and goats: Matthew 25:32
Why have You forsaken Me: Mark 15:34
God works for good: Romans 8:28
Paul and Barnabas split: Acts 15:39–41

CHAPTER 4: DIVORCE IS ADULTERY?

Key text: Mark 10:2–12
Grace and truth: John 1:14
Moses' instructions on divorce: Deuteronomy 24:1–4
Marriage as God established it: Genesis 1:27; 2:24
Duties of husbands and wives: Ephesians 5:22–33
Divorce because of adultery: Matthew 5:32
Divorce because of desertion: 1 Corinthians 7:15
Wives and husbands to submit and love: Ephesians 5:22, 25
Ministry of reconciliation: 2 Corinthians 5:18
John the Baptist and Herod: Mark 6:14–29
Lust is adultery: Matthew 5:28
Burning with passion: 1 Corinthians 7:9
Calling of singleness and chastity: 1 Corinthians 7:25–35
No condemnation: Romans 8:1
New covenant for forgiveness of sins: Matthew 26:28

CHAPTER 5: NO MARRIAGE IN HEAVEN?

Key text: Mark 12:18–27
Sadducees deny resurrection: Acts 23:8
Today with Me in paradise: Luke 23:43
Released from law of marriage: Romans 7:2
Marriages depicts Christ and Church: Ephesians 5:31–32; 5:25
In eternity, no need to multiply: Genesis 1:28
In eternity, no need to combat loneliness: Genesis 2:18; Revelation 21:4
Resurrection: 1 Corinthians 15:12–28; Daniel 12:2; Job 19:25–26
God of Abraham, Isaac, and Jacob: Exodus 3:6
God does not abandon you: Psalm 16:10
Never leave you nor forsake you: Hebrews 13:5

CHAPTER 6: MAKE FRIENDS BY UNRIGHTEOUS WEALTH?

Key text: Luke 16:1–9
Jesus calls His disciples friends: John 15:13, 15
Questionable behavior in parables: Matthew 13:44; 25:1–13
Shrewdness: Matthew 7:24; Ephesians 5:16; Luke 10:27;
   Matthew 10:16; Luke 16:11; Acts 5:29
Qualities of David's army: 1 Chronicles 12:30, 32–33

CHAPTER 7: NO RICH PEOPLE ALLOWED IN HEAVEN?

Key text: Mark 10:17–27
Wealthy believers in the Bible: Genesis 13:2; 26:13;
   30:43; 1 Kings 3:13; 4:26; Job 42:12; Matthew 27:57;
   2 Samuel 19:32
Abraham's bosom: Luke 16:22
Jesus' poverty: Luke 8:3; 9:58; 2 Corinthians 8:9
Solomon on wealth: Ecclesiastes 5:19
Money-related parables: The two debtors (Luke
   7:40–48); the sower (Matthew 13:3–9); the hidden
   treasure (Matthew 13:44); the pearl of great value
   (Matthew 13:45–46); new and old treasures
   (Matthew 13:51–52); the unmerciful servant (Matthew
   18:23–35); the Good Samaritan (Luke 10:30–37); the rich
   fool (Luke 12:16–21); building a tower (Luke 14:28–30);
   the lost coin (Luke 15:8–10); the prodigal son (Luke
   15:11–32); the dishonest manager (Luke 16:1–13); the rich
   man and Lazarus (Luke 16:19–31); the laborers in the vine-
   yard (Matthew 20:1–16); the ten minas (Luke 19:11–27);
   the wicked tenants (Matthew 21:33–44); and the talents
   (Matthew 25:14–30)
Jesus' teaching on money: Luke 16:13; Matthew 13:22;
   Luke 6:24; Matthew 6:21

CHAPTER 8: FEAR GOD?

Key text: Luke 12:1–7

Eternal punishment: 2 Thessalonians 1:9; Matthew 25:46

Restoration of all things: Acts 3:21

Appearances of *hell* in the Bible: Matthew 5:22; 5:29; 5:30; 10:28; 16:18; 18:9; 23:15; 23:33; Mark 9:43; 9:45; 9:47; Luke 12:5; James 3:6; 2 Peter 2:4

Appearances of *Hades* in the Bible: Matthew 11:23; Luke 10:15; 16:23; Acts 2:27; 2:31; Revelation 1:18; 6:8; 20:13; 20:14

God wants all to reach repentance: 2 Peter 3:9

Fear the Lord: Psalm 33:8

Jesus' authority: Matthew 28:18

Concern about God's opinion versus people's opinions: Matthew 6:1–18

Tax collectors and sinners: Mark 2:15

Jesus' purpose to please the Father: John 6:38; Matthew 17:5

Jesus' personal hell on the cross: Matthew 27:46

Jesus not abandoned to Hades: Acts 2:31–32

Jesus builds His Church: Matthew 16:18

CHAPTER 9: SENT TO HELL FOR SPEAKING AN INSULT?

Key text: Matthew 5:21–26

Moses banned from Promised Land: Numbers 20:10–12

Jesus came to fulfill Law: Matthew 5:17

Do not sin in anger: Ephesians 4:26

Fools according to God: Psalm 53:1; Matthew 23:17

Out of the heart the mouth speaks: Matthew 12:34

Jesus insulted: Luke 23:2; John 19:3; Luke 22:64

The thief on the cross: Luke 23:41

Sinners forgiven: Luke 23:43; 1 Timothy 1:13–14

No corrupting talk: Ephesians 4:29

CHAPTER 10: CUT OFF YOUR HAND?

Key text: Mark 9:42–50

Deceitfulness of sin: Hebrews 3:13

Sin grows: James 1:14–15

Righteous alternatives for eyes, hands, and feet: Philippians 3:17; Deuteronomy 15:11; Romans 10:15; Matthew 28:19

Causing another to sin: Mark 9:37

Bearing with the weak: Romans 15:1

CHAPTER 11: NO FORGIVENESS FOR THE UNFORGIVING?

Key text: Matthew 6:7–15

Sins completely removed: Psalm 103:12

Parable of the unmerciful servant: Matthew 18:21–35

Jacob and Esau reconciled: Genesis 33

Ministry of reconciliation: 2 Corinthians 5:18

His power in our weakness: 2 Corinthians 12:9; Ephesians 3:20

CHAPTER 12: AN UNFORGIVABLE SIN?

Key text: Mark 3:22–30

God chooses to forget our sins: Hebrews 8:12

The Spirit placed on God's Servant: Isaiah 42:1

Acknowledge or deny Jesus: Matthew 10:32–33

From the heart the mouth speaks: Matthew 12:34

Satan overpowered: Mark 3:27; John 16:11

Compelled to speak of God: Jeremiah 20:9

The Lord is merciful and gracious: Psalm 103:8–12

CHAPTER 13: BE PERFECT?

Key text: Matthew 5:43–48

Come to Jesus for rest: Matthew 11:28

Delivered into God's kingdom: Colossians 1:13–14

Our righteousness versus that of the scribes and Pharisees: Matthew 5:20

Teleios, **often translated as "mature":** 1 Corinthians 14:20; Hebrews 5:14

Perfect and complete: James 1:4

Perfect love: 1 John 4:18

Jesus "made perfect" (completing the work of salvation): Hebrews 5:9

Teleo **(finished) on the cross:** John 19:28, 30

Merciful as our Father is merciful: Luke 6:36

CHAPTER 14: BELIEVE AND RECEIVE?

Key text: Mark 11:20–25

James and John's ambitious request: Mark 10:35–45

"My hour has not yet come": John 2:4

His grace is sufficient: 2 Corinthians 12:9

Abraham and Moses influence God: Genesis 18:22–33; Exodus 32:7–14

Jesus curses a fig tree: Mark 11:12–14

Asking in faith without doubt: James 1:6

CHAPTER 15: DID JESUS CALL A WOMAN A DOG?

Key text: Mark 7:24–30

View of dogs in Bible times: 2 Kings 9:36; Psalm 59:6; Philippians 3:2

"Is Jesus sexist?"

Curing Peter's mother-in-law: Mark 1:30–31

Healing a woman who had been bleeding: Mark 5:25–34

Straightening the stooped woman: Luke 13:10–17

Reviving Jairus's daughter: Mark 5:35–43

Reviving a grieving mother's son: Luke 7:11–17

Poor widow's offering: Mark 12:41–44

Persistent widow: Luke 18:1–8

Five wise virgins: Matthew 25:1–13

Teaching against lust and divorce: Matthew 5:27–32

Woman caught in adultery: John 7:53–8:11

Woman at the well: John 4:1–26

Driving demons out of Mary Magdalene: Luke 8:2

First miracle at Cana: John 2:1–11

On the cross to Mary and John: John 19:26–27

Mary, Martha, and Lazarus: John 11:1–44

First witnesses of His resurrection: Luke 24:1–12

"Is Jesus racist?"

Sent to lost sheep of Israel: Matthew 15:24

Other sheep not of this pen: John 10:16

Visit of the Magi: Matthew 2:1–12

Healing Roman centurion's servant: Luke 7:9

Driving demons out of Gerasene man: Mark 5:19

Healing deaf man in the Decapolis: Mark 7:31–37

Instructing disciples to reach the nations: Matthew 28:19; Acts 1:8

"Dogs" at the cross: Psalm 22:16

Pray and do not lose heart: Luke 18:1

CHAPTER 16: ONLY ONE WAY TO GOD?

Key text: John 14:1–7
The door of the sheep: John 10:7
Access to the Father through Christ: Ephesians 2:18
Not sent to condemn but to save: John 3:17
God desires all to be saved: 1 Timothy 2:4
Everyone who calls on His name will be saved: Romans 10:13
Separation of sheep and goats: Matthew 25:31–46
Forsaken on the cross: Matthew 27:46
All have sinned and fallen short: Romans 3:23–24
Be prepared to give the reason for your hope: 1 Peter 3:15
Make teaching about God attractive: Titus 2:10
Blessed are those who believe without seeing: John 20:29
Abraham's faith: John 8:56; Galatians 3:9
Faith by people of old: Hebrews 11:1–2
Narrow gate: Matthew 7:13–14

Acknowledgments

This book has taken shape with the help of many wonderful advisers and resources.

Thank you to Zach Zehnder, a gifted author and dynamic leader, for writing such a great foreword. With his expertise on Jesus' words, exhibited in *Red Letter Challenge*, Zach was the ideal person to introduce this book.

Thank you to my initial reviewers who took the time to read the manuscript and provide excellent feedback for improving it: Doug Bielefeldt, Keith Fox, Jack Goldberger, Alice Klement, Gary Larsen, Dan Mueller, and Melody Smith.

Thank you to my family for your constant love and support. Ashley, you have a masterful insight into people—how they think, what they need, what connects with them. Your wise input helps me to refine ideas and relate them to everyday life. I'm grateful for a beautiful wife who has a passion for excellence in all things. Caleb, Ethan, Emma, and Zachary, you bring me so much joy every day! You keep life fun and give me a great sense of purpose. Dad, Mom, and Kelly, you've always championed me as a writer and follower of Jesus. Your enthusiasm propels me forward with confidence.

Thank you to the talented team at Concordia Publishing House, especially those who worked with this manuscript, Laura Lane and Jamie Moldenhauer.

To the saints of Shepherd of the Hills Lutheran Church, School, and Child Care: It's a joy to explore God's Word with you every week. Your love for Jesus and His teachings is a powerful motivator for a preacher!